Physical Character
Pyrenean Moun
(from The Kennel Club t

C000079240

Body: Broad chest reaching just below elbows; sides slightly rounded, rib cage extended well to rear. Good length back, broad, muscular, straight, level.

Hindquarters: Broad muscular loins, fairly prominent haunches, slightly sloping rump, topline curving smoothly into tail. Strongly made double dewclaws on each hind leg.

Tail: Thick at root, tapering gradually towards tip, tip preferably slightly curled; reaching below hocks, thickly coated with fairly long hair forming attractive plume.

Colour: (a) Mainly white with patches of badger, wolf-grey or pale yellow, or (b) White.

Size: Minimum shoulder height: Dogs 70 cms (27.5 ins); Bitches 65 cms (25.5 ins).

Feet: Short and compact, toes slightly arched, strong nails.

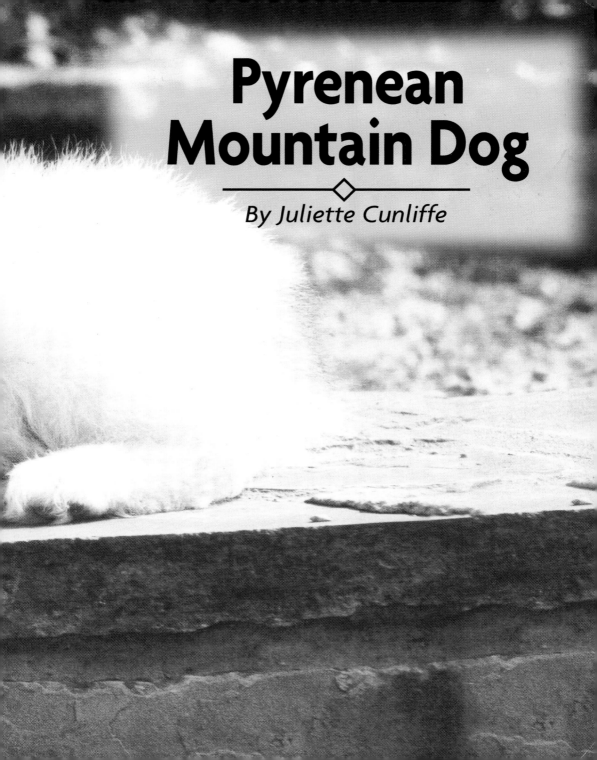

Pyrenean Mountain Dog

◇

By Juliette Cunliffe

CONTENTS

PUBLISHED IN THE UNITED KINGDOM BY:

INTERPET
PUBLISHING
Vincent Lane, Dorking, Surrey RH4 3YX England

ISBN 1-84286-059-3

Photographs by Isabelle Francais and Carol Ann Johnson, with additional photography by: Norvia Behling, TJ Calhoun, Carolina Biological Supply, David Dalton, Doskocil, James Hayden-Yoav, James R Hayden, RBP, Bill Jonas, Dwight R Kuhn, Dr Dennis Kunkel, Mikki Pet Products, Phototake, Jean Claude Revy, Dr Andrew Spielman, Michael Trafford and Alice van Kempen.

The publisher wishes to thank Gale B. Armstrong, Giovanni & Roberta Lazzeri Cardini, Marie-Claude Couty, Rhonda Dalton, Raymond Ducrey, Mrs Beryl Lordy, Rocco Muraca, Michèle Etienne Serclèrat, Mrs Janet Srodzinski and the rest of the owners of the dogs featured in this book.

History of the
PYRENEAN MOUNTAIN DOG

The Pyrenean Mountain Dog is known by several different names, but all of these names are derived from the Pyrenean mountain range in the Basque country, lying between Spain and France. It is in this mountainous region that the breed has long been used as a guardian for flocks of sheep and goats, working on steep slopes, in dense undergrowth and open pasture. The breed was widely used in this manner until the late 19th century, when large predators were eliminated from the region.

In the breed's homeland, the Pyrenean Mountain Dog was used to guard animals from bears and wolves, so it was important that this magnificent breed not only was of great size but also had strength and stamina. Temperament, too, was incredibly important. There could be no nervousness, and yet no amount of aggression could be permitted.

Large Pyrenean-type dogs can

be traced back to well before the birth of Christ, for fossil remains have been found dating back to the Bronze Age (1800–1000 BC). It is believed that large, primarily white guardian dogs, the early ancestors of the Pyrenean breed, migrated from Asia Minor into Europe, both by sea and by land. By sea, the Phoenician traders went from Cadiz to Spain, and then into the Pyrenees; by land, the dogs moved westward with the Aryan migration into Europe, thus helping to establish various different breeds, each of which developed its own individual

Nina Scott Langley's renowned painting (circa 1930) of a Pyrenean Mountain Dog created interest in the breed outside the Basque country where stretch the Pyrenean Mountains.

Facing page: A creation of the Basques, the Pyrenean Mountain Dog is a unique, magnificent dog who is known as le Chien de Montagne des Pyrénées in its homeland and as the Great Pyrenees in the US.

The Maremma Sheepdog, sometimes referred to as the Maremmano-Abruzzese, derives from the Abruzzi Mountains in Italy. The Maremma closely resembles the Pyrenean breed, but is somewhat smaller.

characteristics. Among these were the Maremma, Hungarian Kuvasz, Komondor, Slovensky Cuvac, Polish Tatra Mountain Dog, Anatolian Shepherd Dog, Akbash and Pyrenean Mastiff, the latter clearly a close relation of the Pyrenean Mountain Dog.

Once in Spain, the climatic conditions under which the Pyrenean Mountain Dog developed were similar to those of its native land, and these dogs remained in isolated mountainous regions until the Mediaeval period. An interesting early reference to the breed is a sculptured bas-relief, found over the North Gate of Carcassone, which bears the royal arms of France.

From French writings of 1407, we learn that 'Great Dogs of the Mountains' were used to guard the Chateau of Lourdes. Here they were regularly used as guards for the men making their rounds, and provision was even made for them in the sentry boxes. The Dauphin, Louis XIV, adopted the breed as the Royal Dog of France in 1675, and this caused the breed to be highly sought after by French nobility.

Already these dogs were recognised for their usefulness, for they had both a good sense of smell and exceptionally good eyesight. Whatever their use, be it as flock guardian, pack animal or messenger, one Pyrenean

> **GENUS *CANIS***
> Dogs and wolves are members of the genus *Canis*. Wolves are known scientifically as *Canis lupus* while dogs are known as *Canis domesticus*. Dogs and wolves are known to interbreed. The term *canine* derives from the Latin derived word *Canis*. The term 'dog' has no scientific basis but has been used for thousands of years. The origin of the word 'dog' has never been authoritatively ascertained.

Mountain Dog was considered to be equal to two men.

MOVEMENT TO THE AMERICAS

Pyrenean dogs travelled to Newfoundland with Basque fishermen in 1662. They went as companion animals, but also as guardians. In Newfoundland, the Curly-Coated Retriever was already a favourite of English settlers in that land. The Pyreneans mated with these dogs, bringing about the Landseer Newfoundland, which is a large black and white dog.

THE NINETEENTH CENTURY

Britain's Queen Victoria, a well-known dog lover who did so

much to draw attention to the breeds of dog she owned, had a Pyrenean Mountain Dog in 1850. By the mid-1880s, the breed was registered with the English Kennel Club and was shown at London's Crystal Palace. In France, the breed had been exhibited in the Zoological Gardens of the Bois de Bologne, on the outskirts of Paris, in 1863.

In 1897, Count H A Graff van Bylandt included the breed in his encyclopaedia, *Les Races de Chiens*, published in Brussels. In this, and in the 1904 edition,

there were photographs of this majestic breed, hitherto unknown to so many dog fanciers, and the result was a sudden demand for

The Pyrenean Shepherd Dog (called the Berger des Pyrenees in France) has worked in association with the Pyrenean Mountain Dog for many generations in the Basque country. This smaller breed herds the flock, while the Pyrenean Mountain Dog guards from human and lupine marauders.

The Hungarian Komondor belongs to the family of large white flock guardians. The breed is distinctive for its completely corded coat and its take-charge personality.

puppies. However, in France, this did not have a positive effect on the breed, for in a few short years much of the best breeding stock had been sold abroad, causing a drain on genetic resources and consequently putting the future of the breed in danger.

The first Pyrenean Mountain Dog known in Ireland arrived in Dublin in 1898, having travelled over from France.

EUROPE IN THE EARLY TWENTIETH CENTURY

It was in 1907 that the Pastoure Club was formed in Hautes Pyrénées, France, with the aim of perpetuating interest in the breed. This led to the first breed standard's being published. Two years later, in 1909, Lady Sybil Grant, daughter of Lord Roseberry, brought Pyrenean Mountain Dogs

THE GRANDE MADAME

Madame Harper Trois-Fontaines' de Fontenay kennel was undisputedly the fountainhead of the breed in Britain, providing stock from which many Pyrenean enthusiasts were able to build their kennels, both at home and abroad. This remarkable lady died in 1972, in her ninety-eighth year.

One of the lesser known flock guards, the Tatra Mountain Dog, known as the Owczarek Podhalanski in Poland, is related to the mountain guards of Rumania and Hungary. It is a large, confident breed used to protect flocks as well as estates.

to England, these for the purpose of breeding. In the early 1920s, Sir Cato Worsfold also attempted to establish the breed in Britain, but, like Lady Sybil Grant, without significant success.

Unfortunately, during the 1920s, the Pyrenean Mountain Dog declined both in numbers and in quality in France, but M Senac Lagrange and a handful of other dedicated breeders worked hard to revive the breed. Together they formed the Reunion des Amateurs de Chiens Pyrénéens, and this club drew up the breed standard in the mid-1920s. The club still exists today, and its breed standard has been the foundation stone for all breed standards of the modern era.

In England, it was not until the early 1930s that Mme Jeanne

BRAIN AND BRAWN

Since dogs have been inbred for centuries, their physical and mental characteristics are constantly being changed to suit man's desires for hunting, retrieving, scenting, guarding and warming their masters' laps. During the past 150 years, dogs have been judged according to physical characteristics as well as functional abilities. Few breeds can boast a genuine balance between physique, working ability and temperament.

Harper Trois-Fontaines began her de Fontenay Kennel, which from 1938 was near Amersham in Buckinghamshire. She had first been impressed by the Pyrenean Mountain Dogs she had seen at the Manoir de Careil, when on holiday in France with her husband. He suggested that she order a couple, which she did, no doubt willingly, but these did not arrive in Britain until 1933. Unfortunately, they were not allowed to be quarantined together, and they are said both to have died of loneliness before the age of six months. The following year, Madame successfully brought in a ten-month-old puppy from the Loire, and she thought

HELPING THE ST. BERNARD
Because the number of St. Bernards had been seriously depleted due to avalanches and distemper at the hospice in Switzerland, in 1870 the blood of Pyrenean Mountain Dogs, and that of other large breeds, was used to help the St. Bernard breed back to recovery.

The Kuvasz from Hungary is not as large as its cousin, the Komondor, and enjoys growing popularity in the UK and America.

Take note of this gentle giant. At a dog show in Paris (circa 1930), a Pyrenean Mountain Dog became a press spectacular. This photo appeared in numerous publications of the day.

publicity work on behalf of the breed, not only through dog shows but also with appearances on stage, screen and television. From her kennel, Pyrenean Mountain Dogs were to be exported world-wide.

It appears that it was the late Baron Rothschild who first suggested starting a breed club, this at a tea party at his home in Tring. Seemingly, the very next morning, Mme Harper Trois-Fontaines went to The Kennel Club to obtain registration papers, and opened a bank account for the club. In 1936, the Pyrenean Mountain Club of Great Britain was registered with The Kennel Club (although it was to be almost a decade before the club was officially recognised), and, in October of that year, the first breed classes were judged by France's M Senac Legrange at Crystal Palace.

very highly of this dog, Kop de Careil. Six months later, the bitch Iannette de Boisy joined him, forming the foundation stock of the renowned de Fontenay kennel.

Madame Harper Trois-Fontaines aimed to import only the most typical bloodlines from France, and in this she spared no expense. She also did valuable

BREED NAMES AND NICKNAMES

Known in Britain and some European countries as the Pyrenean Mountain Dog, the breed has various names around the world. In the USA, the breed is known as the Great Pyrenees and, in France, is called Le Chien de Montagne des Pyrénées or Le Chien des Pyrénées. Over 200 years ago, it was also known as the 'King of Sheepdogs' and the 'White-furred Lord.'

DID YOU KNOW?

French writers of the 18th century told their readers that, at Versailles, the Pyrenean dog hunted wolf and wild pig, working alongside scent- and sighthounds.

FROM WORLD WAR II ONWARD

Throughout out the years of World War II, Mme Harper Trois-Fontaines continued in her efforts to get the new breed club recognised by The Kennel Club, and over a period of four years managed to register 150 Pyreneans. Membership increased after the war and, in 1945, The Kennel Club gave the club official recognition, allowing Challenge Certificates to be awarded. It was headed by the same staunch lady supporter of the breed who was at that point its President, Secretary and Treasurer, though this had not been case in its formative years. In May 1946, the breed's very first Championship Show was held at Buckingham Gate in London.

Later, due to the controversy surrounding one person's holding three such posts in the breed club, Madame resigned as Secretary and Treasurer. Subsequently the club ran into difficulties, only to be bailed out financially for the second time by Mme Harper Trois-Fontaines. In 1969, the first Pyrenean Symposium was held, with the aim of furthering knowledge about every aspect of the breed.

The Pyrenean Club of Great Britain still exists, and is one of four clubs now in Britain. In 1996, a Diamond Jubilee Banquet was held, together with the first World Congress, which took place at Coventry. This was an opportunity for enthusiasts from all over the world to get together and share their ideas about the breed, and there was a plentiful supply of knowledgeable speakers from as far apart as Scandinavia and Australia.

THE PYRENEAN AS A CARTING DOG

Pyrenean Mountain Dogs were used for pulling small carts until fairly recent times. This was particularly so in Belgium and northern France, where they delivered milk, like many other of the carting dogs. Although today the subject of carting causes

Mountain Dogs photographed in the Pyrenean Mountains early in the 20th century illustrate the type of working dog that existed about 100 years ago.

controversy in some circles, some breed enthusiasts still use their dogs to pull small, light-weight carts as a hobby.

PYRENEANS AS LIVESTOCK GUARDIANS

This breed's original role in the Pyrenean Mountain region was that of livestock guardian, but now in many countries the Pyrenean Mountain Dog is kept purely as a companion and show dog. However, in some countries, the breed is still employed successfully for its original purpose. A livestock guardian dog is neither a hunter nor a shepherd, but it does show a protective attitude toward its stock and will fend off predators from the animals that it considers as its own property.

In the US, toward the close of the 1970s, there was renewed interest in using the Pyrenean as a livestock guardian dog as new methods of preventing the loss of stock to predators were needed. Among various breeds consid-ered, the Pyrenean was found to be well suited to the job. It had kept its original instincts, yet still showed good-natured behaviour with people, and so made an admirable family companion.

In recent years, Pyrenean Mountain Dogs performed an interesting exercise in Norway, close to the borders of Russia and Finland, where bears were entering a village. A long-standing Norwegian breeder of Pyreneans worked in co-operation with the Norwegian environmental organisation, which placed six puppies on three farms. This understandably caused some concern among breeders, who thought the breed would run the risk of obtaining a bad reputation, thereby losing its popularity as a family dog.

Although the dogs used had chased foxes, it was not known whether they would apply the same principles to chasing off bears. The outcome, however, was that the dogs were indeed effective, showing a high fighting spirit around the bears and completing their mission without injury. Despite resistance from the bears, the dogs maintained their interest in their work and could cope with physical contact with the bears without sustaining injury or becoming nervous. Added to this, they took their own responsibility for livestock in their neighbourhood; on two occasions of accidental encoun-ters with bears, the dogs showed guarding attitudes towards their owners, scaring off the bears.

One of the farmers was so impressed that he subsequently took on two Pyrenean Mountain Dogs of his own. Soon after, although bears were still found at the northern and southern ends of the village, they did not enter

Slovak Cuvac is the Czech equivalent to the Pyrenean Mountain Dog. It is a large white guardian breed utilised to protect flocks in the Liptok Mountains. Rarely seen outside the Czech Republic, the breed is sometimes called Slovensky Tchouvatch.

the village centre, as they had done in previous years.

THE GREAT PYRENEES IN AMERICA

The first pair of Pyrenean Mountain Dogs was introduced to America in 1824 by General Lafayette, who took two males to J S Skinner, author of *The Dog and the Sportsman*. Although there were a few imports following these, the breed in the US was really launched when the Basquaerie Kennel was founded in Massachusetts in 1931. This

was the largest kennel of the breed ever established, and stock produced from this source provided many smaller kennels, both in the US and abroad, with dogs.

In 1933 the Great Pyrenees (as the breed is known in the US) was given official recognition by the American Kennel Club. By April of that year, there was separate classification for the breed at shows. In 1935, the breed standard, which had been based on the French standard of the 1920s, was revised, remaining

unchanged for a further 55 years. Today in the US, the Great Pyrenees is found in the show ring but is also much-loved as a companion in the home; the breed is also used on farms and ranches as a livestock guardian.

PYRENEANS IN NEW ZEALAND
Pyreneans from England's de Fontenay Kennels went to New Zealand in the late 1940s. Early in the next decade, two Pyreneans from the Pondtail Kennel were imported and kept at Auckland Zoo, the latter producing a small litter. However, it was not until 1956 that the breeding of Pyrenean Mountain Dogs began in earnest in New Zealand. There were imports

An example of a Pyrenean Mountain Dog that works for the military is M Dretzen's Ch Porthos, photographed in 1907.

Two Pyrenean Mountain Dogs photographed in the early 1930s. The dog on the left was a dog well known in its day, Ch Thora.

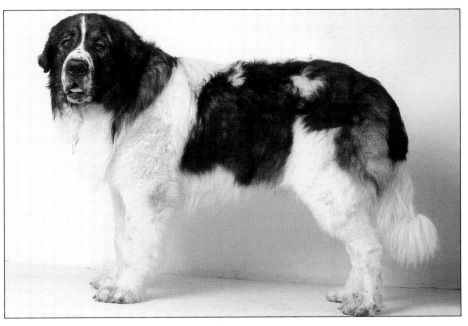

A breed of increasing importance in Spain is the Mastin del Pireneo, known in English-speaking countries as the Pyrenean Mastiff. Unlike most of the other large flock guards, the Mastin del Pireneo can be seen in white with grey, black, brindle or orange. The breed is long-coated, unlike its cousin the Mastin Español.

from Britain in the 1950s and 1960s, but there are some sad stories among them, due primarily to the long journey involved and the time spent in quarantine.

There was a poor survival rate in litters whelped, and the selection of stock from which to breed was limited, so numbers did not increase greatly. Despite this, some Pyreneans went to Australia at this time. In New Zealand, the breed became firmly established in the 1970s and 1980s, with imports from England and also from Australia. The first NZ Champion was Cherryglen Elizabeth, an import from Britain, and it was she who produced the first two NZ-bred champions.

Over recent years, breeders have continued to import stock from prominent kennels in Britain, the US and Australia, but the number of kennels in New Zealand can be counted on two hands. Nonetheless, Pyrenean Mountain Dogs always attract the crowds when they are seen in public, and apart from winning at Group level at dog shows, they can also be seen collecting for charity. Because New Zealand has no natural predators, there is little use for dogs as livestock guardians in the country—although Pyreneans always seem ready to take over the supervision of a few sheep in a paddock if the opportunity arises.

Characteristics of the
PYRENEAN MOUNTAIN DOG

WHY THE PYRENEAN MOUNTAIN DOG?

The Pyrenean Mountain Dog is undoubtedly a magnificent animal, one that has a deep devotion to its family and home, but also an inborn instinct to guard and protect. When considering whether or not this is the dog for them, would-be owners should also take into account the great size of this breed. As a puppy, a Pyrenean is a loveable little ball of fluff, but it will quickly grow into a very large dog. Thus, it will need environmental surroundings to suit, and an owner must be physically capable of handing such a powerful dog. The owner must be able to provide the dog with a large, securely fenced area for sufficient exercise.

Choice of a breed with a profuse light-coloured coat is also something to be taken into account, for a Pyrenean Mountain Dog with a dirty ungroomed coat looks very different from the

Are you ready to enter into the world of the Pyrenean Mountain Dog? 'They don't call me the Great Pyrenees for nothing!'

beautifully presented animal with which one may be familiar from seeing in the show ring.

PERSONALITY

This is an intelligent breed that is trustworthy and affectionate. Although gentle and tractable, Pyrenean Mountain Dogs will be protective of those they consider their 'property,' as well as protective of their territory. As watchdogs, they certainly command respect, but they also make wonderful pets and are very devoted to their families and

Facing page: The Pyrenean's height is usually measured at *its* shoulders—not yours! This is a mountain of a dog that requires a committed, capable owner to love.

homes, needing regular love and attention.

This is a natural guard, capable of and willing to protect flocks and shepherds, originally from wolves and bears. It should always be borne in mind that Pyreneans were bred to be left alone in the mountain valleys with sheep, and that their guarding ability is instinctive, not a result of training. This is a dog that was bred to work alone, without taking commands from people; as such, their personality is rather different from that of most breeds. They can sometimes be rather wilful and, although there are undoubtedly a few Pyrenean Mountain Dogs who take part in obedience, in general they

The Pyrenean Mountain Dog was bred to work alone, protecting the flocks from wolves and bears. They thrive on outdoor work and responsibility as well as companionship and proper care.

are not easily trained to obedience. Many Pyreneans are very independent and do not necessarily give importance to the same things as humans might!

The breed standard says that the breed should be 'quietly confident,' pointing out that 'nervousness and unprovoked aggression are highly undesirable.' This is especially important in such a large breed, for a Pyrenean Mountain Dog with untypical instability of temperament would be extremely difficult to control.

Although boisterous up to the age of about two, once a Pyrenean Mountain Dog has reached full maturity it will be placid by nature and calm around the home. It likes its life to be consistent and predictable, and will enjoy quiet periods in which it may rest comfortably and sleep undisturbed.

In common with other livestock guarding breeds,

A NATURAL GUARD

This is a guarding breed, and consequently it is only natural that Pyreneans cannot be expected to welcome unwanted visitors! Although not 'attack' dogs, their very size and demeanour can be intimidating. However, they will be ready to accept anyone who has been invited to the home. It is therefore important for owners to treat this breed's natural guarding instinct in a responsible manner.

Pyrenean Mountain Dogs will bark, and some owners feel that they do so especially at night. This is one of several reasons for this breed's being best suited to country living, or certainly to a home with understanding neighbours.

PHYSICAL CHARACTERISTICS

This is a breed of great size, substance and power. It looks immensely strong and is well balanced, while the attractive coat and splendid head impart a degree of elegance.

SIZE

Although the breed standard stipulates a minimum height of 70 cms (27.5 ins) at shoulder for dogs and 65 cms (25.5 ins) for bitches, many are considerably taller than this. This is perfectly in order, provided that type and character are retained.

WEIGHING A LARGE BREED

A Pyrenean Mountain Dog is a big breed to weigh, so one cannot use the more usual method of weighing yourself while holding the dog and then subtracting your own weight to obtain the difference. A solution is to use two sets of scales. Stand the dog's front legs on one scale and the hind legs on the other, and then add up the two weights. This shouldn't be too difficult, if your Pyrenean will stand still!

EXERCISE AND AFFECTION
Pyrenean Mountain Dogs need substantial outside exercise areas, but they thrive on love and affection and need to play an important part in the home lives of their owners. Pyreneans left alone, without companionship, become lonely and bored, and bored dogs can become destructive ones.

Weight needs to be in proportion to height, for the Pyrenean Mountain Dog is a powerful animal with great strength. This means, however, that dogs should not carry excess fat. The minimum weight expected for dogs and bitches at the lowest end of the height spectrum is 50 kgs (110 lbs) and 40 kgs (88 lbs), respectively.

Even though the Pyrenean Mountain Dog is a good house dog and is very happy around the home, because of the breed's great size it is imperative that it also has access to a substantial outside area for exercise. Because it is the breed's instinct to patrol its territory, the area to which it is confined should be well fenced, or it will patrol the very limits.

HEAD, EYES AND EARS
The head of the Pyrenean Mountain Dog is strong, but in no way coarse, and should not be too heavy in relation to the dog's size. The top of the head has a definite curve, giving a domed effect. The Kennel Club breed standard gives a clear description of the head features and relevant proportions.

The almond-shaped eyes are a beautiful dark amber-brown in colour. The eyelids should not droop, but should be close-fitting and bordered with black, just as the nose pigment is black. The fairly small ears are triangular in shape, with rounded tips. Although they normally lie flat against the head, they may be slightly raised when the dog is alert.

TAIL
The Pyrenean Mountain Dog's tail is thickly coated with rather long hair, forming a most attractive plume. When in repose, the tail is carried low, the tip turning slightly to one side; when interested, the tail rises and curls

high above the back in a circle when the dog is fully alert.

Movement

Pyrenean Mountain Dogs generally move in an unhurried fashion, steady and smooth, but are well capable of producing bursts of speed when they deem it necessary. When moving slowly, this breed has a tendency to pace, which means that the left fore and hind legs advance in unison, followed by the right fore- and hind legs, and so on.

Coat and Colour

The Pyrenean Mountain Dog's stunning coat is surely one of many attractive features of this majestic breed. There is a profuse undercoat of fine hairs, while the outer coat is of coarser texture. The outer coat is thick, and though it may be straight or slightly wavy, it should never be curly nor fuzzy. Around the neck and shoulders, the coat forms a mane, which is usually less developed in bitches, and the coat is longer toward the tail. The forelegs are fringed, and the long, woolly hair behind the thighs gives the effect of pantaloons. Bitches tend to be more smooth-coated than males.

This breed is predominantly white in colour, but there may be patches of badger, wolf-grey or pale yellow. If present, colour patches may be on the head, ears

HEAVY AND HEAVIER

We all know that Pyrenean Mountain Dogs are large, heavy dogs, but if you try to coax a Pyrenean into something he doesn't want to do, he only seems to get heavier! It has been said that on the first day at a training class, a Pyrenean weighs as much as a small elephant. When trying to teach the down/stay in an obedience class, the dog's weight is that of a Sumo wrestler. And if one tries to administer a pill or cut toenails, the Pyrenean can resemble a Moray eel!

Teeth still in place but slightly worn down in this bitch over ten years old.

or base of tail, and a few are permissible on the body. Black patches that go right down to the root of the hair are highly undesirable.

Maintaining a good, healthy, clean coat on a Pyrenean Mountain Dog is important, so a thorough brushing and combing session is needed about three times each week. Pyreneans do shed their coats, so owners must be prepared to find lots of white hairs around the home and on their clothes! In general, dogs

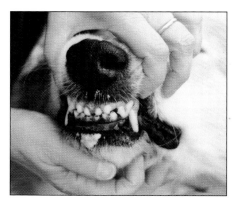

drop their coats just once each year, and bitches twice, usually following their seasons.

MOUTH AND TEETH
Generally, the Pyrenean Mountain Dog has a scissor bite, in which the upper teeth closely overlap the lower ones; this is the typical mouth formation for most canines. However, a pincer bite, in which the teeth meet edge to edge, is also tolerated in this breed. It is important that the teeth are strong, healthy and even (although the two central lower incisors may be set a little deeper than the others), and dentition should be complete. Lips should be close-fitting, and the roof of the mouth and the lips are either black or heavily marked with black. It is interesting to note that, because of the tight-fitting lip formation, the Pyrenean Mountain Dog does not drool or salivate as much as many of the other giant breeds.

BOREDOM SPELLS TROUBLE

A Pyrenean Mountain Dog that is left alone in the home will almost certainly become bored, and a large, bored dog can become a highly destructive one! A bored Pyrenean may decide to chew, and he will probably not take into account which are and which are not your favourite possessions, so be forewarned.

FEATURES OF THE FEET

A rather unusual feature of this breed is that Pyrenean Mountain Dogs have strong double dewclaws on their hind legs. This is something that is required by the breed standard, so is a necessity for exhibition purposes. They should be two completely separate claws, which can be clearly distinguished as two separate toes. It is important that dewclaws be trimmed regularly, as they do not wear down naturally. Although the reason for the breed's having double dewclaws is not certain, it is believed that they may have had a 'snow-shoe' effect. Pyreneans usually have single dewclaws on the front feet, and occasionally these, too, are double. The feet themselves are short and compact, with slightly arched toes and strong nails.

HEALTH CONSIDERATIONS

All breeds encounter health problems of one sort or another, but the Pyrenean Mountain Dog is

THE GENTLE GIANT
Despite its imposing size, the Pyrenean Mountain Dog is of a gentle nature, and is especially good with children. Its size in comparison with that of a small child should, however, be borne in mind when introductions are made, and one should always be aware that until the age of about two, Pyreneans can be rather boisterous.

basically a very healthy breed with few major problems. As time moves on, and as genetic research progresses, clubs dedicated to the breed have begun to conduct health surveys. It is therefore to be expected that more and more problems will come to light, and this can only be for the future benefit of the breed.

To be forewarned is to be forearmed, so the following section of this chapter is not

The strong double dewclaws on the hind legs are, in fact, two additional toes. They should be present.

DO YOU KNOW ABOUT HIP DYSPLASIA?

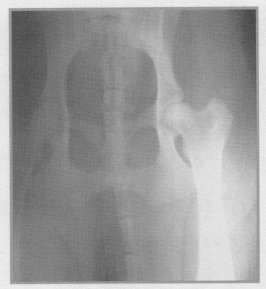

X-ray of a dog with 'Good' hips.

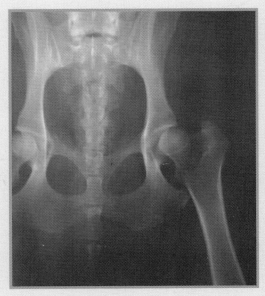

X-ray of a dog with 'Moderate' dysplastic hips.

Hip dysplasia is a fairly common condition found in pure-bred dogs. When a dog has hip dysplasia, its hind leg has an incorrectly formed hip joint. By constant use of the hip joint, it becomes more and more loose, wears abnormally and may become arthritic.

Hip dysplasia can only be confirmed with an x-ray, but certain symptoms may indicate a problem. Your dog may have a hip dysplasia problem if it walks in a peculiar manner, hops instead of smoothly runs, uses its hind legs in unison (to keep the pressure off the weak joint), has trouble getting up from a prone position or always sits with both legs together on one side of its body.

As the dog matures, it may adapt well to life with a bad hip, but in a few years the arthritis develops and many dogs with hip dysplasia become cripples.

Hip dysplasia is considered an inherited disease and only can be diagnosed definitively when the dog is two years old. Some experts claim that a special diet might help your puppy outgrow the bad hip, but the usual treatments are surgical. The removal of the pectineus muscle, the removal of the round part of the femur, reconstructing the pelvis and replacing the hip with an artificial one are all surgical interventions that are expensive, but they are usually very successful. Follow the advice of your veterinary surgeon.

intended to put fear into those who are considering becoming owners of Pyrenean Mountain Dogs. Instead I hope it will help to enlighten them, so that any health problems encountered can be dealt with as early as possible and in the most appropriate manner.

HIP DYSPLASIA

HD, as it is commonly known, is a problem involving the malforma-tion of the ball-and-socket joint at the hip, a developmental condition caused by the interac-tion of many genes. This results in looseness of the hip joints and, although not always painful, it can cause lameness and can impair typical movement.

Hip dysplasia is not a major problem within the breed, but a few cases do occur and some breeders have their dogs' hips scored, as such scoring is now available in most countries. Both hips are tested and scored individually; the lower the score, the less the degree of dysplasia.

Clearly, it is sensible that serious thought be given to using dogs with high scores in breeding programmes, and elimination from a breeding programme may have to be considered. It is worth bearing in mind that a Pyrenean Mountain Dog is a particularly large breed to x-ray, so some breeders feel it wise to discuss with their vets exactly how this is

DO YOU WANT TO LIVE LONGER?

If you like to volunteer, it is wonderful if you can take your dog to a nursing home once a week for several hours. The elder community loves to have a dog with which to visit, and often your dog will bring a bit of companionship to someone who is lonely or somewhat detached from the world. You will be not only bringing happiness to someone else but also keeping your dog busy—and we haven't even mentioned the fact that it has been discovered that volunteering helps to increase your own longevity!

SLEEPING ARRANGEMENTS

A warm, dry place to sleep is essential for a Pyrenean Mountain Dog. Most seem to prefer to sleep on a hard surface, rather than on a carpet, but a Pyrenean will usually not take exception to his owner's comfortable bed! This can be somewhat of an inconvenience, especially if one's Pyrenean snores, which some do.

to be done so that as true a reading as possible can be obtained.

Although a dog's environment does not actually cause hip dysplasia, this may have some bearing on how unstable the hip joint eventually becomes. Osteoarthritis can eventually develop as a result of the instability.

BONE GROWTH

As this is a very large breed, with rapid bone growth, young puppies should not have much lead work on hard pavements; this can lead to problems later in life. Of course they may have short walks, for they will need to become accustomed to their leads, but exercise of this kind must be restricted up to the age of about one year. Most breeders, however, allow their youngsters as much free exercise as they want, although the pups should not be permitted to jump down from high levels.

SKIN PROBLEMS AND ALLERGIES

Some Pyrenean Mountain Dogs seem rather susceptible to skin problems and allergies, although this, of course, is by no means unique to this breed. The reasons behind these problems can be many-fold.

Damp coats can play an important part here, for skin trouble can result if coats are not dried thoroughly. It is also important to groom out any old coat, especially during a moult, for this can also give rise to skin problems.

A common allergy is that to flea saliva and flea bites, making it doubly important that your dog is not plagued by these unwanted parasites. Obviously dogs that have access to farmland may pick up the occasional tick, so owners must be on the lookout for these unwanted creatures too!

Another type of skin irritation, known as a 'hot spot,' often contains a small brown dry spot

TAKING CARE
Science is showing that as people take care of their pets, the pets are taking care of their owners. A study in 1998, published in the *American Journal of Cardiology,* found that having a pet can prolong his owner's life. Pet owners generally have lower blood pressure, and pets help their owners to relax and keep more physically fit. It was also found that pets help to keep the elderly connected to their communities.

in its centre. It is important that owners do not allow infection to set up as a result.

EYE PROBLEMS
The most frequent eye problem found in the Pyrenean Mountain Dog is distichiasis, in which extra hairs grow along the edge of the eyelid and rub along the surface of the cornea. Generally, a young dog grows out of this condition with maturity; as the face 'fills out,' the offending eyelashes are pulled away from the eye, causing no further problem. Obviously, veterinary attention should be sought should the matter not rectify itself as a youngster grows older.

RARELY ENCOUNTERED PROBLEMS
A very few Pyrenean Mountain Dogs have been known to suffer from patellar luxation, a substan-

dard formation of the knee joint. In mild cases, there may be no evident sign of the problem; more severe cases can be both painful and disabling, and arthritis can develop in the long term.

Another cause of arthritis, which can sometimes be found in older dogs, is when the coat has been left wet following exercise outdoors. It is therefore absolutely essential to dry the coat thoroughly and that it is not allowed to remain damp.

As in other breeds, occasionally bone cancers and other cancers are diagnosed in elderly dogs. Thankfully, gastric torsion (bloat) seems not to be a problem, and heart problems do not arise any more frequently than usual.

The Pyrenean Mountain Dog's eyes should be checked regularly by the veterinary surgeon, and any dogs intended for breeding should be screened before planning a mating.

PYRENEAN MOUNTAIN DOG

INTRODUCTION TO THE BREED STANDARD

The breed standard for the Pyrenean Mountain Dog is set down by The Kennel Club and, like standards for other breeds, can be changed occasionally. Such changes come about usually with guidance from experienced people from within the breed clubs, but it should be understood that in Britain The Kennel Club has the final word as to what is incorporated and in what manner. The Kennel Club's revision of all breed standards in the mid-1980s was in part to create uniformity in terms of layout and content.

It is interesting to look back over breed standards through the years and to note some of the alterations that have taken place over time. Many alterations of recent decades are very subtle; for example, where it had been stated previously that 'Areas of black hair, where the black goes right down to the roots' constituted a

Facing page: The breed standard is the guideline for all breeders, judges and exhibitors. The dog that most closely conforms to the standard, in the judge's opinion, is the dog that will win in the show ring.

serious fault, it now states that 'black patches going right down to the root' are 'highly undesirable.'

When discussing the history of the breed, you will recall that attention was attracted by van Bylandt's description of the Pyrenean Mountain Dog in his encyclopaedia *Les Races de Chiens*. This book was a much enlarged 'second' edition, published in 1897, with a subsequent edition in 1904. Although the wording used then was much more scant, much of the description, in essence, has the same meaning. However, a few comments will surely raise

The gait of the Pyrenean Mountain Dog is as vital to the breed as its physical conformation and temperament. The breed should move with an unhurried, steady and smooth gait.

the odd eyebrow, such as that the muzzle was 'rather snipey.' There was also quite a difference in colour, for the section on colour read, 'All white. (Sometimes small orange patches on the ears.)' Height then ranged from 26 to 30 inches, and weight was given as 135 to 155 lbs.

All breed standards are designed effectively to paint a picture in words, though each reader will almost certainly have a slightly different way of interpreting these words. After all, when all is said and done, were everyone to interpret a breed's standard in exactly the same way, there would only be one consistent winner within the breed at any given time!

In any event, to fully comprehend the intricacies of a breed, reading words alone is never enough. In addition, it is essential for devotees to watch other Pyrenean Mountain Dogs being judged at shows and, if possible, to attend seminars at which the breed is discussed. This enables owners to absorb as much as possible about their chosen breed of dog. 'Hands on' experience, providing an opportunity to assess the structure of dogs, is always valuable, especially for those who hope ultimately to judge the breed.

A breed standard undoubtedly helps breeders to produce stock that comes as close as possible to

THE IDEAL SPECIMEN

According to The Kennel Club, 'The Breed Standard is the "Blueprint" of the ideal specimen in each breed approved by a governing body, e.g. The Kennel Club, the Fédération Cynologique Internationale (FCI) and the American Kennel Club.

'The Kennel Club writes and revises Breed Standards taking account of the advice of Breed Councils/Clubs. Breed Standards are not changed lightly to avoid "changing the standard to fit the current dogs" and the health and well-being of future dogs is always taken into account when new standards are prepared or existing ones altered.'

the recognised standard, and helps judges to know exactly what they are looking for. This enables a judge to make a carefully considered decision when selecting the most typical Pyrenean Mountain Dog present to head his line of winners.

However familiar one is with the breed, it is always worth refreshing one's memory by re-reading the standard, for it is sometimes all too easy to overlook, or perhaps conveniently forget, certain features.

THE KENNEL CLUB STANDARD FOR THE PYRENEAN MOUNTAIN DOG

General Appearance: Great size, substance and power; looking immensely strong and well balanced. A certain elegance imparted by attractive coat and correct head.

Characteristics: A natural guard dog protecting shepherd and sheep.

Temperament: Quietly confident. Nervousness and unprovoked aggression highly undesirable.

BREEDING CONSIDERATIONS

The decision to breed your dog is one that must be considered carefully and researched thoroughly before moving into action. Some people believe that breeding will make their bitches happier or that it is an easy way to make money. Unfortunately, indiscriminate breeding only worsens the rampant problem of pet overpopulation, as well as putting a considerable dent in your pocketbook. As for the bitch, the entire process from mating through whelping is not an easy one and puts your pet under considerable stress. Last, but not least, consider whether or not you have the means to care for an entire litter of pups. Without a reputation in the field, your attempts to sell the pups may be unsuccessful.

Head and Skull: Strong head without coarseness, not too heavy in relation to size of dog. Top, seen from front and side, definitely curved to give domed effect. Breadth at widest point about equal to length from occiput to stop. Sides nearly flat and of good depth. No obvious stop, only slight furrow, so that skull and muzzle are joined by gentle slope. Strong muzzle, medium length, slight taper near tip. Nose black. Head seen from above has form of a blunt V, well filled in below eyes.

Eyes: Almond shaped, dark amber-brown. Close-fitting eyelids set somewhat obliquely, bordered with black. Drooping lower lids undesirable. Intelligent and contemplative expression.

Ears: Fairly small, triangular, rounded tips. Root level with eyes. Normally lie flat against head, may be slightly raised when alert.

Mouth: Complete dentition, healthy, strong and even. Scissor bite correct, i.e. upper teeth closely overlapping lower teeth and set square to the jaws, but pincer bite tolerated. Two central lower incisors may be set a little deeper than others. Close-fitting lips, upper just covering lower. Roof of mouth and lips black or heavily marked with black.

Neck: Fairly short, thick and muscular. Some dewlap permitted.

Forequarters: Powerful shoulders lying close to body. Medium angulation between shoulder blade and upper arm. Forelegs straight, heavily boned, well muscled. Elbows not too close to chest, nor too far off, giving adequate width of stance and free-striding movement. Pasterns flexible without weakness.

Body: Broad chest reaching just below elbows; sides slightly rounded, rib cage extended well to rear. Good length back, broad, muscular, straight, level. Dogs usually have more pronounced waist than bitches, giving greater curve to lower body.

Hindquarters: Broad muscular loins, fairly prominent haunches, slightly sloping rump, topline curving smoothly into tail. Very strong heavily muscled thighs tapering gradually to strong hocks. Stifle and hock of medium angulation seen from side. Strongly made double dewclaws on each hind leg; lack of this identifying characteristic totally undesirable. The hind feet may turn out slighty but legs themselves must be straight.

Feet: Short and compact, toes slightly arched, strong nails.

Tail: Thick at root, tapering gradually towards tip, tip prefer-ably slightly curled; reaching below hocks, thickly coated with fairly long hair forming attractive plume. Carried low in repose, with tip turned slightly to one side. Tail rises as dog becomes interested: curled high above back in a circle when fully alert.

Gait/Movement: Unhurried, steady and smooth, as if driven by powerful hindquarters, well within its capacity, yet able to produce bursts of speed. Tends to pace at low speed.

Coat: Profuse undercoat of very fine hairs; outer coat longer, coarser-textured, thick and straight or slightly wavy, never curly or fuzzy. Longer towards tail and forming mane round neck and shoulders. Forelegs fringed.

Long, very dense woollier hair on rear of thighs giving pantaloon effect. Bitches tend to be smoother-coated than dogs and have less developed mane.

Colour: (a) Mainly white with patches of badger, wolf-grey or pale yellow, or (b) White. (a) and (b) are of equal merit. The colour patches may be on head, ears or base of tail and a few permissible on body. Black patches going right down to the roots highly undesirable. Black nose and eyerims; liver or pink pigmentation highly undesirable.

Size: Minimum shoulder height: Dogs 70 cms (27.5 ins); Bitches 65 cms (25.5 ins). Most will considerably exceed this, great size is essential provided type and character are retained. Minimum weight: dogs: 50 kgs (110 lbs); bitches: 40 kgs (88 lbs); these weights apply only to specimens of minimum height, taller ones should be heavier. Weight always in proportion to height, giving a powerful dog of great strength, but excess weight due to fat undesirable.

Faults: Any departure from the foregoing points should be considered a fault and the seriousness with which the fault should be regarded should be in exact proportion to its degree.

Note: Male animals should have two apparently normal testicles descended into the scrotum.

The Pyrenean Mountain Dog possesses a profuse undercoat of fine hairs and a coarser outer coat, coloured solid white, with patches of yellow, wolf-grey and/or badger on the head, ears and base of tail. In the US, most dogs are solid white with very few markings.

PYRENEAN MOUNTAIN DOG

HOW TO SELECT A PUPPY

Before reaching the decision that you will definitely look for a Pyrenean Mountain Dog puppy, it is essential that you are clear in your mind that this is absolutely the most suitable breed for you and your family. A puppy grows rapidly and the breed's great size will undoubtedly be one of the first things to take into account, as your home environment and surroundings must be suitable. A Pyrenean Mountain Dog usually reaches full height by about ten months, but continues to develop bodily until the age of two-and-a-half years.

Also take into account that the white coat will shed, especially when moulting, so it is inevitable that you will find long white hairs around your home and on your clothes.

The temperament is quietly confident and usually very stable, but one should not lose sight of the fact that the Pyrenean Mountain Dog also has a natural guarding instinct. It is essential therefore that any puppy showing signs of nervousness or unprovoked aggression is avoided.

Such temperament is very rare in the breed, and is never to be encouraged.

Once you are certain that this is the breed for you, you must also ask yourself why you want a Pyrenean Mountain Dog; do you want one purely as a pet or as a show dog? This should be made clear to the breeder when you make your initial enquiries. If you are seeking a potential show dog, you will need to take the breeder's advice as to which available puppy shows the most promise for the show ring. If looking for a pet, you should discuss your family situation with the breeder and take his advice as to which puppy is likely to suit best. The average litter for the Pyrenean is

At nine weeks of age, this dynamic mountain duo are ready to begin their lives with their new families.

Facing page: Locating a qualified, proven breeder is tantamount to finding the Pyrenean puppy of your dreams. These two six-week-old angels are destined to make two owners' dreams come true. Breeder, Beryl Lord (Laudley).

six puppies, but they can have litters as large as 12 or even more; thus, selection will be considerable once you've located a breeder and litter.

When you have your first opportunity to visit the most potentially suitable litter, watch the puppies interact together. You will find that different puppies

PUPPY SELECTION

Your selection of a good puppy can be determined by your needs. A show potential or a good pet? It is your choice. Every puppy, however, should be of good temperament. Although show-quality puppies are bred and raised with emphasis on physical conformation, responsible breeders strive for equally good temperament. Do not buy from a breeder who concentrates solely on physical beauty at the expense of personality.

PREPARING FOR PUP

Unfortunately, when a puppy is bought by someone who does not take into consideration the time and attention that dog ownership requires, it is the puppy who suffers when he is either abandoned or placed in a shelter by a frustrated owner. So all of the 'homework' you do in preparation for your pup's arrival will benefit you both. The more informed you are, the more you will know what to expect and the better equipped you will be to handle the ups and downs of raising a puppy. Hopefully, everyone in the household is willing to do his part in raising and caring for the pup. The anticipation of owning a dog often brings a lot of promises from excited family members: 'I will walk him every day,' 'I will feed him,' 'I will house-train him,' etc., but these things take time and effort, and promises can easily be forgotten once the novelty of the new pet has worn off.

have different personalities, and some will be more boisterous and extroverted than others. Although you will need to use your own judgement as to which one is most likely to fit in with your lifestyle, if the breeder you have selected is a good one, you will also be guided by his or her judgement and knowledge of his dogs.

You should have done plenty of background research on the breed, and preferably have visited a few breed club or Championship Shows. Shows give you an opportunity to see the breed in some numbers, plus the chance to observe the dogs with their breeders and owners.

Remember that the dog you select should remain with you for the duration of its life, which will hopefully be ten or more years, so making the right decision from the outset is of utmost importance. No dog should be moved from one home to another simply because its owners were thoughtless enough not to have done sufficient 'homework' before selecting the breed. It is always important to remember that, when looking for a puppy, a good breeder will be assessing you as a prospective new owner just as

The author, Juliette Cunliffe, making the acquaintance of an handsome nine-week-old puppy.

carefully as you are selecting the breeder.

Puppies almost invariably look enchanting, but you must select one from a caring breeder who has given the puppies all the attention they deserve, and has looked after them well. The puppy you select should look well fed, but not pot-bellied, as this might indicate worms. Eyes should look bright and clear, without discharge. The nose should be moist, which is an indication of good health, but should never be runny. It goes

YOUR SCHEDULE . . .

If you lead an erratic, unpredictable life, with daily or weekly changes in your work requirements, consider the problems of owning a puppy. The new puppy has to be fed regularly, socialised (loved, petted, handled, introduced to other people) and, most importantly, allowed to visit outdoors for toilet training. As the dog gets older, it can be more tolerant of deviations in its feeding and toilet relief.

DOCUMENTATION

Two important documents you will get from the breeder are the pup's pedigree and registration certificate. The breeder should register the litter and each pup with The Kennel Club, and it is necessary for you to have the paperwork if you plan on showing or breeding in the future.

Make sure you know the breeder's intentions on which type of registration he will obtain for the pup. There are limited registrations which may prohibit the dog from being shown, bred or competing in non-conformation trials such as Working or Agility if the breeder feels that the pup is not of sufficient quality to do so. There is also a type of registration that will permit the dog in non-conformation competition only.

On the reverse side of the registration certificate, the new owner can find the transfer section, which must be signed by the breeder.

too noticeable on a young puppy, but will become more evident as the puppy gets older.

Gender differences in the breed may also affect your choice of a puppy. Do you want a male or a female? In the Pyrenean Mountain Dog, males are generally larger and carry more coat than females, especially around the mane. Males are not usually tolerant of each other unless they have been raised together, so males often need to be kept separately.

Something else to consider is whether or not to take out veterinary insurance. Vet's bills can mount up, and you must always be certain that sufficient funds are available to give your dog any veterinary attention that may be

INSURANCE

Many good breeders will offer you insurance with your new puppy, which is an excellent idea. The first few weeks of insurance will probably be covered free of charge or with only minimal cost, allowing you to take up the policy when this expires. If you own a pet dog, it is sensible to take out such a policy as veterinary fees can be high, although routine vaccinations and boosters are not covered. Look carefully at the many options open to you before deciding which suits you best.

without saying that there should certainly be no evidence of loose motions, nor of parasites. The puppy you choose should also have a healthy-looking coat, an important indication of good health internally. Always check the bite of your selected puppy to be sure that it is neither overshot nor undershot. This may not be

needed. Keep in mind, though, that routine vaccinations will not be covered.

SELECTING A BREEDER

If you are convinced that the Pyrenean Mountain Dog is the ideal dog for you, it's time to learn about where to find a puppy and what to look for. Locating a litter of Pyrenean Mountain Dogs should not present a problem for the new owner. You should enquire about breeders in your area who enjoy a good reputation in the breed. You are looking for an established breeder with outstanding dog ethics and a strong commitment to the breed. New owners should have as many questions as they have doubts. An established breeder is indeed the

one to answer your four million questions and make you comfortable with your choice of the Pyrenean Mountain Dog. An established breeder will sell you a puppy at a fair price if, and only if, the breeder determines that you are a suitable, worthy owner of his dogs. An established breeder can be relied upon for advice, no matter what time of day or night. A reputable breeder will accept a puppy back, without questions, should you decide that this is not the right dog for you.

When choosing a breeder, reputation is much more important than convenience of location. Do not be overly impressed by breeders who run brag advertisements in the presses about their stupendous champions. The real quality breeders are quiet and unassuming. Take advantage of resources available at the shows and from The Kennel Club.

Besides the eventual size difference between the male and female, there are other temperamental and behavioural differences to consider. Discuss gender with your chosen breeder.

PUPPY PERSONALITY

When a litter becomes available to you, choosing a pup out of all those adorable faces will not be an easy task! Sound temperament is of utmost importance, but each pup has its own personality and some may be better suited to you than others. A feisty, independent pup will do well in a home with older children and adults, while quiet, shy puppies will thrive in a home with minimal noise and distractions. Your breeder knows the pups best and should be able to guide you in the right direction.

Choosing a breeder is an important first step in dog ownership. Fortunately, the majority of Pyrenean Mountain Dog breeders is devoted to the breed and its well-being. New owners should have little problem finding a reputable breeder who doesn't live on the other side of the country (or in a different country). The Kennel Club is able to recommend breeders of quality Pyrenean Mountain Dogs, as can any local all-breed club or Pyrenean Mountain Dog club.

Once you have contacted and met a breeder or two and made your choice about which breeder is best suited to your needs, it's time to visit the litter. Keep in mind that many top breeders have waiting lists. Sometimes new owners have to wait as long as two years for a puppy. If you are really committed to the breeder whom you've selected, then you will wait (and

It is not uncommon for breeders to have more than one litter in his kennel at one time. These 9-week-old puppies have bonded with this 16-week-old pup. Consider the advantages of acquiring a slightly older puppy that is likely house-trained and more predictable.

> **BOY OR GIRL?**
> An important consideration to be discussed is the sex of your puppy. For a family companion, a bitch may be the better choice, considering the female's inbred concern for all young creatures and her accompanying tolerance and patience. It is always advisable to spay a pet bitch, which may guarantee her a longer life.

hope for an early arrival!). If not, you may have to resort to your second- or third-choice breeder. Don't be too anxious, however. If the breeder doesn't have a waiting list, or any customers, there is probably a good reason. It's no different than visiting a pub with no clientele. The better pubs and restaurants always have waiting lists—and it's usually worth the wait. Besides, isn't a puppy more important than a pint?

Breeders commonly allow visitors to see their litters by around the fifth or sixth week, and puppies leave for their new homes between the eighth and tenth week. Breeders who permit their puppies to leave early are more interested in your pounds than in their puppies' well-being. Puppies need to learn the rules of the pack from their dams, and most dams continue teaching the pups manners and dos and don'ts until around the eighth week.

Breeders spend significant amounts of time with the Pyrenean Mountain Dog toddlers so that the pups are able to interact with the 'other species,' i.e. humans. Given the long history that dogs and humans share, bonding between the two species is natural but must be nurtured. A well-bred, well-socialised Pyrenean Mountain Dog pup wants nothing more than to be near you and please you.

COMMITMENT OF OWNERSHIP

After considering all of these factors, you have most likely already made some very important decisions about selecting your puppy. You have chosen a Pyrenean Mountain Dog, which means that you have decided which characteristics you want in a dog and what type of dog will best fit into your family and lifestyle. If you have selected a breeder, you have gone a step further—you have done your research and found a responsible, conscientious person who breeds quality Pyrenean Mountain Dogs and who should be a reliable source of help as you and your puppy adjust to life together. If you have observed a litter in action, you have obtained a firsthand look at the dynamics of a puppy 'pack' and, thus, you have learned about each pup's individual personality—perhaps you have even found one that

LETTING GO
Breeders rarely release puppies until they are eight to ten weeks of age. This is an acceptable age for most breeds of dog, excepting toy breeds, which are not released until around 12 weeks, given their petite sizes. If a breeder has a puppy that is 12 weeks of age or older, it is likely well socialised and house-trained. Be sure that it is otherwise healthy before deciding to take it home.

particularly appeals to you.

However, even if you have not yet found the Pyrenean puppy of your dreams, observing pups will help you learn to recognise certain behaviour and to determine what a pup's behaviour indicates about his temperament. You will be able to pick out which pups are the leaders, which ones are less outgoing, which ones are confident, which ones

ARE YOU A FIT OWNER?
If the breeder from whom you are buying a puppy asks you a lot of personal questions, do not be insulted. Such a breeder wants to be sure that you will be a fit provider for his puppy.

are shy, playful, friendly, aggressive, etc. Equally as important, you will learn to recognise what an healthy pup should look and act like. All of these things will help you in your search, and when you find the Pyrenean Mountain Dog that was meant for you, you will know it!

Researching your breed, selecting a responsible breeder and observing as many pups as possible are all important steps on the way to dog ownership. It may seem like a lot of effort…and you have not even taken the pup home yet! Remember, though, you cannot be too careful when it comes to deciding on the type of dog you want and finding out about your prospective pup's background. Buying a puppy is not—or should not be—just another whimsical purchase. This is one instance in which you actually do get to choose your own family! You may be thinking that buying a puppy should be fun—it should not be so serious and so much work. Keep in mind that your puppy is not a cuddly stuffed toy or decorative lawn ornament; rather, he is a living creature that will become a real member of your family. You will come to realise that, while buying a puppy can be a pleasurable and exciting endeavour, it is not something to be taken lightly. Relax…the fun will start when the pup comes home!

Always keep in mind that a puppy is nothing more than a baby in a furry disguise…a baby who is virtually helpless in a human world and who trusts his owner for fulfilment of his basic needs for survival. In addition to food, water and shelter, your pup needs care, protection, guidance and love. If you are not prepared to commit to this, then you are not prepared to own a dog.

Wait a minute, you say. How hard could this be? All of my neighbours own dogs and they seem to be doing just fine. Why should I have to worry about all of this? Well, you should not worry about it; in fact, you will probably find that once your Pyrenean pup gets used to his new home, he will fall into his place in the family quite naturally. However, it never hurts to emphasise the commitment of dog ownership. With some time and patience, it is really not too difficult to raise a curious and exuberant Pyrenean Mountain Dog pup to become a well-adjusted and well-mannered adult dog—a dog that could be your most loyal friend.

PREPARING PUPPY'S PLACE IN YOUR HOME

Researching your breed and finding a breeder are only two aspects of the 'homework' you will have to do before taking your Pyrenean Mountain Dog

QUALITY FOOD

The cost of food must be mentioned. All dogs need a good-quality food with an adequate supply of protein to develop their bones and muscles properly. Most dogs are not picky eaters but, unless fed properly, can quickly succumb to skin problems.

puppy home. You will also have to prepare your home and family for the new addition. Much as you would prepare a nursery for a newborn baby, you will need to designate a place in your home that will be the puppy's own. How you prepare your home will depend on how much freedom the dog will be allowed. Whatever you decide, you must ensure that he has a place that he can 'call his own.'

When you bring your new puppy into your home, you are bringing him into what will become his home as well. Obviously, you did not buy a puppy with the intentions of catering to his every whim and allowing him to 'rule the roost,' but in order for a puppy to grow into a stable, well-adjusted dog, he has to feel comfortable in his surroundings. Remember, he is

To introduce a new Pyrenean puppy into an household that contains older resident dogs, supervision, control and encouragement will be required to keep all family members content and comfortable.

PHOTO COURTESY OF DOSKOCIL

leaving the warmth and security of his mother and littermates, as well as the familiarity of the only place he has ever known, so it is important to make his transition as easy as possible. By preparing a place in your home for the puppy, you are making him feel as welcome as possible in a strange new place. It should not take him long to get used to it, but the sudden shock of being transplanted is somewhat traumatic for a young pup. Imagine how a small child would feel in the same situation—that is

how your puppy must be feeling. It is up to you to reassure him and to let him know, 'Little chap, you are going to like it here!'

WHAT YOU SHOULD BUY

CRATE

To someone unfamiliar with the use of crates in dog training, it may seem like punishment to shut a dog in a crate, but this is not the case at all. Although all breeders do not advocate crate training, more and more breeders and trainers are recommending crates as preferred tools for show puppies as well as pet puppies.

Crates are not cruel—crates have many humane and highly effective uses in dog care and training. For example, crate training is a popular and successful house-training method. In addition, a crate can keep your dog safe during travel and, perhaps most importantly, a crate provides your dog with a place of his own in your home. It serves as a 'doggie bedroom' of sorts—your Pyrenean Mountain Dog can curl up in his crate when he wants to sleep or when he just needs a break. Many dogs sleep in their crates overnight. With soft bedding and his favourite toy, a crate becomes a cosy pseudo-den for your dog. Like his ancestors, he too will seek out the comfort and retreat of a den—you just happen to be providing him with

CRATE TRAINING TIPS

During crate training, you should partition off the section of the crate in which the pup stays. If he is given too big an area, this will hinder your training efforts. Crate training is based on the fact that a dog does not like to soil his sleeping quarters, so it is ineffective to keep a pup in a crate that is so big that he can eliminate in one end and get far enough away from it to sleep. Also, you want to make the crate den-like for the pup. Blankets and a favourite toy will make the crate cosy for the small pup; as he grows, you may want to evict some of his 'roommates' to make more room.

It will take some coaxing at first, but be patient. Given some time to get used to it, your pup will adapt to his new home-within-a-home quite nicely.

The size of the crate is another thing to consider. Puppies do not stay puppies forever—in fact, a Pyrenean puppy can virtually grow right before your eyes! A small crate may be fine for a very young Pyrenean Mountain Dog pup, but it will not do him much good for long. Unless you have the money and the inclination to buy a new crate every time your pup has a growth spurt, it is better to get one that will accommodate your dog both as a pup and at full size. Pyrenean Mountain Dogs require the largest crates available, known as 'giant' size.

BEDDING

Veterinary bedding in the dog's crate will help the dog feel more at home, and you may also like to pop in a small blanket. First, this will take the place of the leaves, something more luxurious than what his early ancestors enjoyed.

As far as purchasing a crate, the type that you buy is up to you. It will most likely be one of the two most popular types: wire or fibreglass. There are advantages and disadvantages to each type. For example, a wire crate is more open, allowing the air to flow through and affording the dog a view of what is going on around him, while a fibreglass crate is sturdier. Both can double as travel crates, providing protection for the dog.

Breeders will acclimate the litter to ex-pens and crates as a part of the pups' basic education. Puppies that are accustomed to being confined will more readily accept crate training in their new homes.

PLAY'S THE THING

Teaching the puppy to play with his toys in running and fetching games is an ideal way to help the puppy develop muscle, learn motor skills and bond with you, his owner and master.

He also needs to learn how to inhibit his bite reflex and never to use his teeth on people, forbidden objects and other animals in play. Whenever you play with your puppy, you make the rules. This becomes an important message to your puppy in teaching him that you are the pack leader and control everything he does in life. Once your dog accepts you as his leader, your relationship with him will be cemented for life.

twigs, etc., that the pup would use in the wild to make a den; the pup can make his own 'burrow' in the crate. Although your pup is far removed from his den-making ancestors, the denning instinct is still a part of his genetic makeup. Second, until you take your pup home, he has been sleeping amid the warmth of his mother and litter-mates, and while a blanket is not the same as a warm, breathing body, it still provides heat and something with which to snuggle. You will want to wash your pup's bedding frequently in case he has a toileting 'accident' in his crate, and replace or remove any blanket that becomes ragged and starts to fall apart.

Toys

Toys are a must for dogs of all ages, especially for curious playful pups. Puppies are the 'children' of the dog world, and what child does not love toys? Chew toys provide enjoyment for both dog and owner—your dog will enjoy playing with his favourite toys, while you will enjoy the fact that they distract him from chewing on your expensive shoes and leather sofa. Puppies love to chew; in fact, chewing is a physical need for pups as they are teething, and everything looks appetising! The full range of your possessions— from old tea towel to Oriental carpet—are fair game in the eyes of a teething pup. Puppies are not all that discerning when it comes to finding something literally to 'sink their teeth into'—everything tastes great!

Pyrenean Mountain Dog puppies are fairly aggressive chewers and only the hardest, strongest toys should be offered to them. Large, hard rubber balls and sturdy chew-bones are suitable.

Breeders advise owners to resist stuffed toys, because they can become de-stuffed in no time. The overly excited pup may ingest the stuffing, which is neither digestible nor nutritious. Similarly, squeaky toys are quite popular, but must be avoided for the Pyrenean Mountain Dog. Perhaps a squeaky toy can be used as an aid in training, but not for free play. If a pup 'disembowels' one of these, the small plastic squeaker inside can be dangerous if swallowed.

Be careful of natural bones, which have a tendency to splinter into sharp, dangerous pieces. Also be careful of rawhide, which can turn into pieces that are easy to swallow and become a mushy mess on your carpet.

Monitor the condition of all your pup's toys carefully and get rid of any that have been chewed to the point of becoming potentially dangerous.

TOYS, TOYS, TOYS!

With a big variety of dog toys available, and so many that look like they would be a lot of fun for a dog, be careful in your selection. It is amazing what a set of puppy teeth can do to an innocent-looking toy, so, obviously, safety is a major consideration. Be sure to choose the most durable products that you can find. Hard nylon bones and toys are a safe bet, and many of them are offered in different scents and flavours that will be sure to capture your dog's attention. It is always fun to play a game of catch with your dog, and there are balls and flying discs that are specially made to withstand dog teeth.

LEAD

A nylon lead is probably the best option, as it is the most resistant to puppy teeth should your pup take a liking to chewing on his lead. Of course, this is a habit that should be nipped in the bud, but, if your pup likes to chew on his lead, he has a very slim chance of being able to chew through the strong nylon. Nylon leads are also lightweight, which is good for a young Pyrenean Mountain Dog who is just getting used to the idea of walking on a lead. For everyday walking and safety purposes, the nylon lead is a good choice. As your Pyrenean gets larger and stronger, you may want to purchase a thicker lead, such as one made of sturdy leather. Of course, there are leads designed for training purposes but these are not necessary for routine walks.

COLLAR

Your pup should get used to wearing a collar all the time since you will want to attach his ID tags to it; plus, you have to attach the lead to something! A nylon collar is a good choice for a puppy. Make certain that the collar fits snugly enough so that the pup cannot wriggle out of it, but is loose enough so that it will not be uncomfortably tight around the pup's neck. You should be able to fit a finger between the pup's neck and the collar. It may take some time for your pup to get used to wearing the collar, but soon he will not even notice that it is there. Again, you may want to purchase a thicker, stronger collar as the pup grows. Choke collars are made for training, but are not recommended for use on heavily-coated dogs.

FOOD AND WATER BOWLS

Your pup will need two bowls, one for food and one for water. You may want two sets of bowls, one for indoors and one for outdoors, depending on where the dog will be fed and where he will be spending time. Stainless steel or sturdy plastic bowls are popular choices. Plastic bowls are more chewable, but dogs tend not to chew on the steel variety, which can be sterilised. It is important to buy sturdy bowls since anything is in danger of being chewed by puppy teeth and you do not want your dog to be constantly chewing

CHOOSE AN APPROPRIATE COLLAR

The **BUCKLE COLLAR** is the standard collar used for everyday purposes. Be sure that you adjust the buckle on growing puppies. Check it every day. It can become too tight overnight! These collars can be made of leather or nylon. Attach your dog's identification tags to this collar.

The **CHOKE COLLAR** is made for training, but should not be usedon the Pyrenean, as it isharsh and damaging to the heavy coat. It is constructed of highly polished steel so that it slides easily through the stainless steel loop. The idea is that the dog controls the pressure around his neck and he will stop pulling if the collar becomes uncomfortable. It is only used during training and should never be left on a dog.

The **HALTER** is for a trained dog that has to be restrained to prevent running away, chasing a cat and the like. Considered the most humane of all collars, it is frequently used on smaller dogs for which collars are not comfortable.

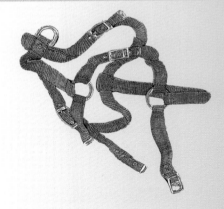

Your local pet shop sells a variety of dishes and bowls suitable for food and water. Get the largest sizes available.

apart his bowl (for his safety and for your purse!).

CLEANING SUPPLIES

Until a pup is house-trained, you will be doing a lot of cleaning. 'Accidents' will occur, which is acceptable in the beginning stages of toilet training because the puppy does not know any better. All you can do is be prepared to clean up any accidents as soon as they happen. Old rags, towels, newspapers and a safe disinfectant are good to have on hand.

BEYOND THE BASICS

The items previously discussed are the bare necessities. You will find out what else you need as you go along—grooming supplies, flea/tick protection, baby gates to partition a room, etc. These things will vary depending on your situation, but it is important that you have everything you need to feed and make your Pyrenean Mountain Dog comfortable in his first few days at home.

PUPPY-PROOFING YOUR HOME

Aside from making sure that your Pyrenean Mountain Dog will be comfortable in your home, you also have to make sure that your home is safe for your Pyrenean Mountain Dog. This means taking precautions that your pup will not get into anything he should not get into and that there is nothing within his reach that may harm him should he sniff it, chew it, inspect it, etc. This probably seems obvious since, while you are primarily concerned with your pup's safety, at the same time you do not want your belongings to be ruined. Breakables should be placed out of reach if your dog is to have full run of the house. If he is to be limited to certain places within the house, keep any potentially dangerous items in the 'off-limits' areas.

An electrical cord can pose a danger should the puppy decide to taste it—and who is going to convince a pup that it would not make a great chew toy? Cords should be fastened tightly against the wall. If your dog is going to spend time in a crate, make sure that there is nothing near his crate that he can reach if he sticks his curious little nose or paws through the openings. Just as you would with a child, keep all household cleaners and chemicals where they cannot be reached.

It is also important to make

It is your responsibility to clean up after your dog has relieved himself. Pet shops have various aids to assist in the cleanup job.

sure that the outside of your home is safe. Of course, your puppy should never be unsupervised, but a pup let loose in the garden will want to run and explore, and he should be granted that freedom. Pyrenean Mountain Dogs can be great escape artists and need very sturdy fencing surrounding their territory. Some are especially good at digging. If a Pyrenean digs a hole in the garden, the hole is best left exactly as it is and not filled in again; otherwise, it will simply reappear!

Do not let a fence give you a false sense of security; you would be surprised at how crafty (and persistent) a dog can be in working out how to dig under and squeeze his way through holes, or

CHEMICAL TOXINS

Scour your garage for potential puppy dangers. Remove weed killers, pesticides and antifreeze materials. Antifreeze is highly toxic and even a few drops can kill even a large dog. The sweet taste attracts the animal, who will quickly consume it from the floor or curbside.

NATURAL TOXINS

Examine your grass and garden landscaping before bringing your puppy home. Many varieties of plants have leaves, stems or flowers that are toxic if ingested, and you can depend on a curious puppy to investigate them. Ask your vet for information on poisonous plants or research them at your library.

to jump or climb over a fence. The remedy is to make the fence well embedded into the ground and, although Pyreneans do not tend to jump over objects, high enough so that it really is impossible for your dog to get over it (about 2 metres should suffice). Be sure to repair or secure any gaps in the fence. Check the fence periodically to ensure that it is in good shape and make repairs as needed; a very determined pup may return to the same spot to 'work on it' until he is able to get through.

FIRST TRIP TO THE VET

You have selected your puppy, and your home and family are ready. Now all you have to do is collect your Pyrenean pup from the breeder and the fun begins, right? Well…not so fast. Something else you need to plan is your pup's first trip to the veterinary surgeon. Perhaps the breeder can recommend someone in the area who specialises in giant breeds, or maybe you know some other Pyrenean Mountain Dog owners who can suggest a good vet. Either way, you should have an appointment arranged for your pup before you pick him up.

The pup's first visit will consist of an overall examination to make sure that the pup does not have any problems that are not apparent to you. The veterinary surgeon will also set up a schedule for the pup's vaccinations; the breeder will inform you of which ones the pup has

PUPPY-PROOFING

Thoroughly puppy-proof your house before bringing your puppy home. Never use cockroach or rodent poisons in any area accessible to the puppy. Avoid the use of toilet cleaners. Most dogs are born with 'toilet sonar' and will take a drink if the lid is left open. Also keep the rubbish secured and out of reach.

already received and the vet can continue from there.

INTRODUCTION TO THE FAMILY

Everyone in the house will be excited about the puppy's coming home and will want to pet him and play with him, but it is best to make the introduction low-key so as not to overwhelm the puppy. He is apprehensive already. It is the first time he has been separated from his mother and the breeder, and the ride to your home is likely to be the first time he has been in a car. The last thing you want to do is smother him, as this will only frighten him further. This is not to say that human contact is not extremely necessary at this stage, because this is the time when a connection between the pup and his human family is formed. Gentle petting and soothing words should help console him, as well as just putting him down and letting him explore on his own (under your watchful eye, of course).

The pup may approach the family members or may busy himself with exploring for a while. Gradually, each person should spend some time with the pup, one at a time, crouching down to get as close to the pup's level as possible, letting him sniff their hands and petting him gently. He definitely needs human attention and he needs to be touched—this is how to form an immediate bond. Just remember that the pup is experiencing many things for the first time, at the same time. There are new people, new noises, new smells and new things to investigate, so be gentle, be affectionate and be as comforting as you can be.

PUP'S FIRST NIGHT HOME

You have travelled home with your new charge safely in his crate. He's been to the vet for a thorough check-up; he's been

The arrival of your Pyrenean puppy will be an exciting time for the whole family. Do not over-whelm your new charge, and introduce him to the family in as low-key a manner as possible.

weighed, his papers have been examined and perhaps he's even been vaccinated and wormed as well. He's met (and licked!) the whole family, including the excited children and the less-than-happy cat. He's explored his area, his new bed, the garden and anywhere else he's been permitted. He's eaten his first

FINANCIAL RESPONSIBILITY

Grooming tools, collars, leashes, dog beds and, of course, toys will be an expense to you when you first obtain your pup, and the cost will continue throughout your dog's lifetime. If your puppy damages or destroys your possessions (as most puppies surely will!) or something belonging to a neighbour, you can calculate additional expense. There is also flea and pest control, which every dog owner faces more than once. You must be able to handle the financial responsibility of owning a dog.

PUPPY PROBLEMS

The majority of problems that are commonly seen in young pups will disappear as your dog gets older. However, how you deal with problems when he is young will determine how he reacts to discipline as an adult dog. It is important to establish who is boss (hopefully it will be you!) right away when you are first bonding with your dog. This bond will set the tone for the rest of your life together.

meal at home and relieved himself in the proper place. He's heard lots of new sounds, smelled new friends and seen more of the outside world than ever before... and that was just the first day! He's worn out and is ready for bed...or so you think!

It's puppy's first night home and you are ready to say 'Good night.' Keep in mind that this is his first night ever to be sleeping alone. His dam and littermates are no longer at paw's length and he's a bit scared, cold and lonely. Be reassuring to your new family member, but this is not the time to spoil him and give in to his inevitable whining.

Puppies whine. They whine to let others know where they are

and hopefully to get company out of it. Place your pup in his new bed or crate in his designated area and close the door. Mercifully, he may fall asleep without a peep. When the inevitable occurs, however, ignore the whining—he is fine. Be strong and keep his interest in mind. Do not allow yourself to feel guilty and visit the pup. He will fall asleep eventually.

Many breeders recommend placing a piece of bedding from the pup's former home in his new bed so that he recognises and is comforted by the scent of his littermates. Others still advise placing a hot water bottle in the bed for warmth. The latter may be a good idea provided the pup doesn't attempt to suckle—he'll

FEEDING TIPS
You will probably start feeding your pup the same food that he has been getting from the breeder; the breeder should give you a few days' supply to start you off. Although you should not give your pup too many treats, you will want to have puppy treats on hand for coaxing, training, rewards, etc. Be careful, though, as a small pup's calorie requirements are relatively low and a few treats can add up to almost a full day's worth of calories without the required nutrition.

HOW VACCINES WORK
If you've just bought a puppy, you surely know the importance of having your pup vaccinated, but do you understand how vaccines work? Vaccines contain the same bacteria or viruses that cause the disease you want to prevent, but they have been chemically modified so that they don't cause any harm. Instead, the vaccine causes your dog to produce antibodies that fight the harmful bacteria. Thus, if your pup is exposed to the disease in the future, the antibodies will destroy the viruses or bacteria.

get good and wet, and may not fall asleep so fast.

Puppy's first night can be somewhat stressful for both the pup and his new family. Remember that you are setting the tone of night-time at your house. Unless you want to play with your pup every night at 10 p.m., midnight and 2 a.m., don't initiate the habit. Your family will thank you, and so will your pup!

PREVENTING PUPPY PROBLEMS

SOCIALISATION

Now that you have done all of the preparatory work and have helped your pup get accustomed to his new home and family, it is about time for you to have some fun! Socialising your Pyrenean pup gives you the opportunity to show off your new friend, and your pup gets to reap the benefits of being an adorable furry creature that people will want to pet and, in general, think is absolutely precious!

A FORTNIGHT'S GRACE

It will take at least two weeks for your puppy to become accustomed to his new surroundings. Give him lots of love, attention, handling, frequent opportunities to relieve himself, a diet he likes to eat and a place he can call his own.

Besides getting to know his new family, your puppy should be exposed to other people, animals and situations. This will help him become well adjusted as he grows up and less prone to being timid or fearful of the new things he will encounter. Luckily, Pyreneans are not generally dog-aggressive though males are less tolerant of other males than are females. Of course, your Pyrenean pup must not come into close contact with dogs you don't know well until his course of injections is complete.

Your pup's socialisation began with the breeder, but now it is your responsibility to continue it. The socialisation he receives until the age of 12 weeks is the most critical, as this is the time when he forms his impressions of the outside world. Be especially careful during the eight-to-ten-week-old period, also known as the fear period. The interaction he receives during this time should be gentle and reassuring. Lack of socialisation, and/or negative experiences during the socialisation period, can manifest itself in fear and aggression as the dog grows up. Your puppy needs lots of positive interaction, which of course includes human contact, affection, handling and exposure to other animals.

Once your pup has received his necessary vaccinations, feel free to take him out and about (on

MANNERS MATTER

During the socialisation process, a puppy should meet people, experience different environments and definitely be exposed to other canines. Through playing and interacting with other dogs, your puppy will learn lessons, ranging from controlling the pressure of his jaws by biting his littermates to the inner-workings of the canine pack that he will apply to his human relationships for the rest of his life. That is why removing a puppy from its litter too early (before eight weeks) can be detrimental to the pup's development.

his lead, of course). Walk him around the neighbourhood, take him on your daily errands, let people pet him, let him meet other dogs and pets, etc. Puppies do not have to try to make friends; there will be no shortage of people who will want to introduce themselves. Just make sure that you carefully supervise each meeting. If the neighbourhood children want to say hello, for example, that is great—children and pups most often make great companions. However, sometimes an excited child can unintentionally handle a pup too roughly, or an overzealous pup can playfully nip a little too hard. You want to make socialisation experiences positive ones. What a

pup learns during this very formative stage will affect his attitude toward future encounters. You want your dog to be comfortable around everyone. A pup that has a bad experience with a child may grow up to be a dog that is shy around or aggressive toward children.

CONSISTENCY IN TRAINING

Dogs, being pack animals, naturally need a leader, or else they try to establish dominance in their packs. When you welcome a dog into your family, the choice of who becomes the leader and who becomes the 'pack' is entirely up to you! Your pup's intuitive quest for dominance, coupled with the fact that it is nearly impossible to look at an adorable Pyrenean pup

Before the puppy is released from the breeder, it should have had some exposure to young people. At the precious age of six weeks, a puppy must be supervised whenever a child is present to ensure that both are on their best behaviour.

PROPER SOCIALISATION

The socialisation period for puppies is from age 8 to 16 weeks. This is the time when puppies need to leave their birth family and take up residence with their new owners, where they will meet many new people, other pets, etc. Failure to be adequately socialised can cause the dog to grow up fearing others and being shy and unfriendly due to a lack of self-confidence.

with his 'puppy-dog' eyes and not cave in, give the pup almost an unfair advantage in getting the upper hand! A pup will definitely test the waters to see what he can and cannot do. Do not give in to those pleading eyes—stand your ground when it comes to disciplining the pup and make sure that all family members do the same. It will only confuse the pup if Mother tells him to get off the sofa when he is used to sitting up there with Father to watch the nightly news. Avoid discrepancies by having all members of the household decide on the rules before the pup even comes home… and be consistent in enforcing them! Early training shapes the dog's

MEET THE WORLD

Thorough sociali-sation includes not only meeting new people but also being introduced to new experiences such as riding in the car, having his coat brushed, hearing the televi-sion, walking in a crowd—the list is endless. The more your pup experiences, and the more positive the experiences are, the less of a shock and the less fright-ening it will be for your pup to encounter new things.

personality, so you cannot be unclear in what you expect.

COMMON PUPPY PROBLEMS

The best way to prevent puppy problems is to be proactive in stopping an undesirable behaviour as soon as it starts. The old saying 'You can't teach an old dog new tricks' does not necessarily hold true, but it is true that it is much easier to discourage bad behaviour in a young developing pup than to wait until the pup's bad behaviour becomes the adult dog's bad habit. There are some problems that are especially prevalent in puppies as they develop.

NIPPING

As puppies start to teethe, they feel the need to sink their teeth into anything available...unfortunately, that usually includes your fingers, arms, hair and toes. You may find this behaviour cute for the first five seconds...until you feel just how sharp those puppy teeth are. Nipping is something you want to discourage immediately and consistently with a firm 'No!' (or whatever number of firm 'Nos' it takes for him to understand that you mean business). Then, replace your finger with an appropriate chew toy. While this behaviour is merely annoying when the dog is young, it can become dangerous as your Pyrenean Mountain Dog's

CHEWING TIPS

Chewing goes hand in hand with nipping in the sense that a teething puppy is always looking for a way to soothe his aching gums. In this case, instead of chewing on you, he may have taken a liking to your favourite shoe or something else which he should not be chewing. Again, realise that this is a normal canine behaviour that does not need to be discouraged, only redirected. Your pup just needs to be taught what is acceptable to chew on and what is off limits. Consistently tell him NO when you catch him chewing on something forbidden and give him a chew toy. Conversely, praise him when you catch him chewing on something appropriate. In this way you are discouraging the inappropriate behaviour and reinforcing the desired behaviour. The puppy chewing should stop after his adult teeth have come in, but an adult dog continues to chew for various reasons—perhaps because he is bored, perhaps to relieve tension or perhaps he just likes to chew. That is why it is important to redirect his chewing when he is still young.

adult teeth grow in and his jaws develop, and he continues to think it is okay to gnaw on human appendages. Your Pyrenean does not mean any harm with a friendly nip, but he also does not know the strength of his large jaws.

STRESS-FREE

Some experts in canine health advise that stress during a dog's early years of development can compromise and weaken his immune system, and may trigger the potential for a shortened life expectancy. They emphasise the need for happy and stress-free growing-up years.

CRYING/WHINING

Your pup will often cry, whine, whimper, howl or make some type of commotion when he is left alone. This is basically his way of calling out for attention to make sure that you know he is there and that you have not forgotten about him. Your puppy feels insecure when he is left alone, when you are out of the house and he is in his crate or when you are in another part of the house and he cannot see you. The noise he is making is an expression of the anxiety he feels at being alone, so he needs to be taught that being alone is okay. You are not actually training the dog to stop making noise; rather, you are training him to feel comfortable when he is alone and thus removing the need for him to make the noise. This is where the crate with cosy bedding and a toy comes in handy.

You want to know that your pup is safe when you are not there to supervise, and you know that he will be safe in his crate rather than roaming freely about the house. In order for the pup to stay in his crate without making a fuss, he first needs to be comfortable in his crate. On that note, it is extremely important that the crate is never used as a form of punishment; this will cause the pup to view the crate as a negative place, rather than as a place of his own for safety and retreat.

Accustom the pup to the crate in short, gradually increasing time intervals in which you put him in the crate, maybe with a treat, and stay in the room with him. If he cries or makes a fuss, do not go to him, but stay in his sight. Gradually he will realise that staying in his crate is all right without your help, and it will not be so traumatic for him when you are not around. You may want to leave the radio on softly when you leave the house; the sound of human voices may be comforting to him.

Quiet socialisation time with the family children will nurture the bond between the Pyrenean puppy and his people.

Puppies that are left alone for long periods can suffer from separation anxiety, punctuated by whining, pouting and alarmingly sad expressions.

PYRENEAN MOUNTAIN DOG

SPECIAL FEEDING CONSIDERATIONS

A Pyrenean Mountain Dog should be fed sensibly on a high-quality diet, but protein content will vary according to whether or not the dog lives an especially active lifestyle. When purchasing a puppy, a carefully selected breeder should be able to give good advice in this regard, but it is generally accepted that dogs leading active lives need more protein than those who spend most of their time by the fireside.

It is difficult to over-feed a Pyrenean puppy, for they get the sensation of feeling full quite quickly. This is not a greedy breed; Pyreneans, in general, tend to eat less in quantity than might be expected for their size. However, correct feeding is very important, especially during the crucial stage of bone growth.

Although Pyreneans are not especially susceptible to excess weight gain, an owner should never be tempted to allow a dog to put on too much weight. An overweight dog is more prone to health problems than one that is of correct weight for its size. Feeding any dog

titbits between meals will run the risk of having an unhealthy, over-weight dog in maturity.

There are now numerous high-quality canine meals available, and one of them is sure to suit your own Pyrenean Mountain Dog. Once again, you should be able to obtain sound advice from your dog's breeder as to which food is considered most suitable. Whether or not you decide to feed a small amount of extra calcium will depend largely on the diet you have chosen; discuss this with your vet. When you buy your puppy, the breeder should provide you with a diet sheet that gives details of exactly how your puppy has been fed. Of course you will be at

A well-cared-for Pyrenean puppy is a happy, smiling companion.

Facing page: All members of the family should be involved in the care and training of the new Pyrenean puppy.

Your new Pyrenean puppy should be offered the same high-quality food that the breeder offered. Should you decide to change the brand, do so very gradually so as not to upset the puppy's system.

liberty to change that food, together with the frequency and timing of meals, as the youngster reaches adulthood, but this should be done gradually.

Some owners still prefer to feed fresh food, instead of one of the more convenient complete diets. However, there are so many of the latter now available, some scientifically balanced, that a lot will depend on personal preference. If one has a 'finicky eater,' although one has to be very careful not to unbalance an otherwise balanced diet, sometimes a little added fresh

meat, or even beef or chicken stock, will gain a dog's interest and stimulate the appetite.

TYPES OF COMPLETE FOOD FOR DOGS

Dog foods are produced in three basic types: dried, semi-moist and tinned. Dried foods are useful for the cost-conscious, for overall they tend to be less expensive than semi-moist or tinned foods. Dried foods also contain the least fat and the most preservatives. In general, tinned foods are made up of 60–70 percent water, while semi-moist ones often contain so much sugar that they are perhaps the least preferred by owners, even though their dogs seem to like them.

When selecting your dog's diet, three stages of development must be considered: the puppy stage, the adult stage and the senior or veteran stage.

PUPPY STAGE

Puppies instinctively want to suck milk from their mother's teats; a normal puppy will exhibit this behaviour just a few moments following birth. If puppies do not attempt to suckle within the first half-hour or so, the breeder should encourage them to do so by placing them on the nipples, having selected ones with plenty of milk. This early milk supply is important in providing the essential colostrum, which protects the puppies during the first eight to ten weeks of their lives. Although a mother's milk is much better than any milk

FEEDING TIP
You must store your dried dog food carefully. Open packages of dog food quickly lose their vitamin value, usually within 90 days of being opened. Mould spores and vermin could also contaminate the food.

TEST FOR PROPER DIET
A good test for proper diet is the colour, odour and firmness of your dog's stool. A healthy dog usually produces three semi-hard stools per day. The stools should have no unpleasant odour. They should be the same colour from excretion to excretion.

formula, despite there being some excellent ones available, if the puppies do not feed, the breeder will have to feed them by hand. For those with less experience, advice from a veterinary surgeon is important so that not only the right quantity of milk is fed but also that of correct quality, fed at suitably frequent intervals, usually every two hours during the first few days of life.

Puppies should be allowed to nurse from their mothers for about the first six weeks, although, starting around the third or fourth week, the breeder will begin to introduce small portions of suitable solid food. Most breeders like to introduce alternate milk and meat meals initially, building up to weaning time.

By the time the puppies are seven or a maximum of eight weeks old, they should be fully weaned and fed solely on a proprietary puppy food. Selection of the most suitable, good-quality diet at this time is essential, for a puppy's fastest growth rate is during the first year of life. From the time a new owner takes a puppy home, the Pyrenean youngster will usually need to be fed three times a day until six months of age. This will then be reduced to twice daily until at least the age of twelve months, and then usually to just one meal. It is always wise not to feed a meal within an hour (before and after) of any strenuous exercise.

A Pyrenean Mountain Dog usually reaches height by about ten months, but continues to develop bodily until the age of two-and-a-half years, so the time when a young Pyrenean is switched to adult food can vary according to the make of food used and to bodily development. Veterinary surgeons are usually able to offer advice in this regard. Puppy and junior diets should be well balanced for the needs of your dog so that, except in certain circumstances, additional vitamins, minerals and proteins will not be required.

QUICKLY FEELING FULL
Perhaps surprisingly, it is difficult to over-feed a Pyrenean Mountain Dog puppy. They seem to feel full quite quickly. If feeding fresh meat in their diet, this breed seems especially to like tripe, for to eat the stomach and intestines is quite natural for them.

ADULT DIETS
A dog is generally considered an adult when it has stopped growing. Again, the Pyrenean Mountain Dog continues to

develop bodily until the age of two-and-a-half years, so you should rely upon your veterinary surgeon or dietary specialist to recommend an acceptable mainte-nance diet based on your dog's individual growth and develop-ment. Major dog food manufac-turers specialise in this type of food, and it is merely necessary for you to select the one best suited to your dog's needs. Active dogs may have different require-ments than sedate dogs.

SENIOR DIETS

As dogs get older, their metabo-lism changes. The older dog usually exercises less, moves more slowly and sleeps more. This change in lifestyle and physiological performance requires a change in diet. Since these changes take place slowly, they might not be recognisable. What is easily recognisable is weight gain. By continuing to feed your dog an adult-maintenance diet when it is slowing down metabolically, your dog will gain weight. Obesity in an older dog compounds the health problems that already accompany old age.

As your dog gets older, few of his organs function up to par. The kidneys slow down and the intestines become less efficient. These age-related factors are best handled with a change in diet and a change in feeding schedule to give smaller portions that are

FOOD PREFERENCE
Selecting the best dried dog food is difficult. There is no majority consensus among veterinary scientists as to the value of nutrient analyses (protein, fat, fibre, moisture, ash, cholesterol, minerals, etc.). All agree that feeding trials are what matter, but you also have to consider the individual dog. The dog's weight, age and activity level, and what pleases his taste, all must be considered. It is probably best to take the advice of your veterinary surgeon. Every dog's dietary require-ments vary, even during the lifetime of a particular dog.

If your dog is fed a good dried food, it does not require supple-ments of meat or vegetables. Dogs do appreciate a little variety in their diets, so you may choose to stay with the same brand but vary the flavour. Alternatively, you may wish to add a little flavoured stock to give a difference to the taste.

more easily digested. Some Pyreneans are never switched to a senior diet, but others are switched over at about seven or eight years of age. There is no single best diet for every older dog. While many dogs do well on light or senior diets, other dogs do better on puppy diets or other special premium diets such as lamb and rice. Be sensitive to your senior Pyrenean Mountain Dog's diet, as this will help control other problems that may arise with your old friend.

GRAIN-BASED DIETS

Some less expensive dog foods are based on grains and other plant proteins. While these products may appear to be attractively priced, many breeders prefer a diet based on animal proteins and believe that they are more conducive to your dog's health. Many grain-based diets rely on soy protein, which may cause flatulence (passing gas).

There are many cases, however, when your dog might require a special diet. These special require-ments should only be recommended by your veterinary surgeon.

WATER

Just as your dog needs proper nutrition from his food, water is an essential 'nutrient' as well. Water keeps the dog's body properly hydrated and promotes normal function of the body's systems. During house-training it is necessary to keep an eye on how much water your Pyrenean Mountain Dog is drinking, but once he is reliably trained he should have access to clean fresh water at all times, especially if you feed dried food. Make certain that the dog's water bowl is clean, and change the water often.

EXERCISE

The Pyrenean Mountain Dog is historically a guardian of sheep and, as such, tends to move at a leisurely pace. However, when they choose to be, Pyreneans can be quick and very agile. Exercise is necessary for both the health and happiness of any dog, as well as for maintenance of a muscular condition. The exercise given depends very much on the home environment, but, if possible, a good walk each day, with plenty of opportunity for free run in a

What are you feeding your dog?

Read the label on your dog food. Many dog foods only advise what 50—55% of the contents are, leaving the other 45% in doubt.

Calcium 1.3%

Fatty Acids 1.6%

Crude Fibre 4.6%

Moisture 11%

Crude Fat 14%

Crude Protein 22%

45.5% ? ? ?

DRINK, DRANK, DRUNK— MAKE IT A DOUBLE

In both humans and dogs, as well as most living organisms, water forms the major part of nearly every body tissue. Naturally, we take water for granted, but without it, life as we know it would cease.

For dogs, water is needed to keep their bodies functioning biochemically. Additionally, water is needed to replace the water lost while panting. Unlike humans, who are able to sweat to dissipate heat, dogs must pant to cool down, thereby losing the vital water from their bodies needed to regulate their body temperatures. Humans lose electrolyte-containing products and other body-fluid components through sweating; dogs do not lose anything except water.

Water is essential always, but especially so when the weather is hot or humid or when your dog is exercising or working vigorously.

safe environment should become routine in adulthood. Please remember, though, that until puppies are a year old, lead work should be very limited, and they should not be allowed to climb up and down stairs nor to jump down from high levels.

Pyreneans need plenty of area in which to exercise freely. Since they also need to be walked on-lead, it is essential that the owner is able to control such a large dog. When allowing a dog to run free, safety is of utmost

'DOES THIS COLLAR MAKE ME LOOK FAT?'

While humans may obsess about how they look and how trim their bodies are, many people believe that extra weight on their dogs is a good thing. The truth is, pets should not be over- or under-weight, as both can lead to or signal sickness. In order to tell how fit your pet is, run your hands over his ribs. Are his ribs buried under a layer of fat or are they sticking out considerably? If your pet is within his normal weight range, you should be able to feel the ribs easily, but they should not protrude abnormally. If you stand above him, the outline of his body should resemble an hourglass. Some breeds do tend to be leaner while some are a bit stockier, but making sure your dog is the right weight for his breed will certainly contribute to his good health.

CHANGE IN DIET
As your dog's caretaker, you know the importance of keeping his diet consistent, but sometimes when you run out of food or if you're on holiday, you have to make a change quickly. Some dogs will experience digestive problems, but most will not. If you are planning on changing your dog's menu, do so gradually to ensure that your dog will not have any problems. Over a period of four to five days, slowly add some new food to your dog's old food, increasing the percentage of new food each day.

importance. For this reason, all possible escape routes should be thoroughly checked out before letting a dog off the lead, and of course one's garden also needs to be safely enclosed by sturdy, high fencing, which should be checked at regular intervals. If one does not wish the dog to have free access to the very extremities of the garden, a good-sized outdoor run should be constructed. Pyrenean Mountain Dogs should never be chained up, unsupervised, outdoors.

When allowing a Pyrenean to have free run in a public area, it is important that he is not allowed to jump up on people. This is such a large breed that an

No exercise compares to a vigorous run on the beach with a worthy chum. Despite the Pyrenean's great size, this is a very active breed that thrives on free running and excitement.

FEEDING TIPS

Dog food must be at room temperature, neither too hot nor too cold. Fresh water, changed daily and served in a clean bowl, is mandatory, especially when feeding dried food.

Never feed your dog from the table while you are eating, and never feed your dog leftovers from your own meal. They usually contain too much fat and too much seasoning.

Dogs must chew their food. Hard pellets are excellent; soups and slurries are to be avoided.

Don't add leftovers or any extras to normal dog food. The normal food is usually balanced, and adding something extra destroys the balance.

Except for age-related changes, dogs do not require dietary variations. They can be fed the same diet, day after day, without becoming ill.

accident could happen, albeit unintentionally. For this reason, sensible training from puppyhood is essential.

Many Pyrenean Mountain Dogs enjoy swimming when given the opportunity, but of course this should only be permitted in a safe environment and under supervision. Some adult Pyreneans also go out hiking with their owners, a few even carrying their very own set of saddle bags!

Bear in mind that an overweight dog should never be suddenly over-exercised; instead he should be encouraged to increase exercise slowly. Not only is exercise essential to keep the dog's body fit, it is essential to his mental well-being. A bored dog will find something to do, which often manifests itself in some type of

DO DOGS HAVE TASTE BUDS?

Watching a dog 'wolf' or gobble his food, seemingly without chewing, leads an owner to wonder whether their dogs can taste anything. Yes, dogs have taste buds, with sensory perception of sweet, salty and sour. Puppies are born with fully mature taste buds.

destructive behaviour. In this sense, exercise is essential for the owner's mental well-being as well!

GROOMING

COAT MAINTENANCE

General grooming of a Pyrenean Mountain Dog's coat is a relatively simple, but necessary, procedure. Because this breed sheds large amounts of coat, grooming should become a very important regular routine that aids in conditioning the coat. Even owners who do not show their dogs should pay attention to the coat about three times each week, giving it a thorough brushing and combing; this should be done daily during a moult.

Each owner will have his own preferences for the best type of grooming equipment to use, so you would be wise to discuss this with your breeder when buying your puppy. There are now many excellent pet stores in the majority of countries, and of course the widest range of equipment can be found on sale at major Championship Shows.

A slicker brush is good for initially removing any debris from the coat, while a steel rake, slicker brush or wide-toothed comb will help to remove any loose hairs from the undercoat. This will be a particularly

GROOMING EQUIPMENT
How much grooming equipment you purchase will depend on how much grooming you are going to do. Here are some basics:
• Slicker brush
• Steel rake
• Nylon bristle brush
• Natural bristle brush
• Metal comb
• Blaster
• Rubber mat
• Dog shampoo
• Spray hose attachment
• Ear cleaner
• Cotton wipes
• Towels
• Nail clippers

important part of the grooming procedure when the coat is moulting, at which time the coat will need attention every day. A bristle with nylon brush can then be used to go over the entire coat, finishing off by using the slicker brush again. Obviously, head hair should be dealt with gently, and a soft, natural bristle brush is good for this area.

BATHING
How frequently you bath your Pyrenean Mountain Dog will depend very much on your dog's lifestyle, and whether or not you show your dog. Your dog will need to be exercised in all types

Your local pet shop will have the tools necessary for the proper grooming of your Pyrenean. Get the best quality, as you'll be using them frequently and want them to last for a long time.

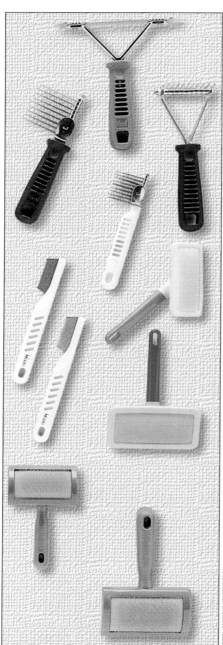

PHOTO COURTESY OF MIKKI PET PRODUCTS.

of weather, and in wet weather the chances are that your dog will need to be not only dried off thoroughly upon return but also cleaned up! From time to time, you will almost inevitably need to bath your dog, or at least to freshen up the legs, especially around the elbows, and under the belly. A dry shampoo can be useful on the remainder of the coat. Prior to bathing, some owners like to use cornflour sprinkled into the coat and then

DEADLY DECAY

Did you know that periodontal disease (a condition of the bone and gums surrounding a tooth) can be fatal? Having your dog's teeth and mouth checked yearly can prevent it.

brushed out, as this helps to remove some of the dirt.

Like most anything, if you accustom your pup to being bathed as a puppy, it will be second nature by the time he grows up. You want your dog to be at ease in the bath or else it could end up a wet, soapy, messy ordeal for both of you!

Brush your Pyrenean Mountain Dog thoroughly before wetting his coat. This will get rid of most mats and tangles, which are harder to remove when the coat is wet. Make certain that your dog has a good non-slip surface on which to stand. Begin by wetting the dog's coat, checking the water temperature to make sure that it is neither too hot nor too cold. A shower or hose attachment is necessary for thoroughly wetting and rinsing the coat.

Next, apply shampoo to the dog's coat and work it into a good lather. Wash the head last, as you do not want shampoo to drip into the dog's eyes while you are washing the rest of his body. You should use only a shampoo that is made for dogs. Do not use a product made for human hair. Work the shampoo all the way down to the skin. You can use this opportunity to check the skin for any bumps, bites or other abnormalities. Do not neglect any area of the body—get all of the hard-to-reach places.

Once the dog has been

The puppy should welcome the feeling of a soft nylon brush on its coat.

Acclimated to grooming by its breeder, your puppy will hopefully be the handsome model of patience and glamour that this puppy is.

Keep grooming sessions short and sweet, lest your Pyrenean will lose heart.

A wide-toothed comb, applied to the undercoat during shedding, will limit the amount of Pyrenean hair that floats around your home.

Protect his eyes from the shampoo by shielding them with your hand and directing the flow of water in the opposite direction. You should also avoid getting water in the ear canal. Be prepared for your dog to shake out his coat— you might want to stand back, but make sure you have a hold on the dog to keep him from running through the house.

EAR CLEANING

The ears should be kept clean with a cotton wipe and ear cleaner made especially for dogs. Do not probe into the ear canal with a cotton bud, as this can cause injury. Be on the lookout for any signs of infection or ear mite infestation. If your Pyrenean Mountain Dog has been shaking his head or scratching at his ears frequently, this usually indicates a problem. If the dog's ears have an unusual odour, this is a sure sign of mite infestation or infection, and a signal to have his ears checked by the veterinary surgeon.

It is important that ears are never allowed to remain damp, as this can encourage fungus and mite infestation. A dry ear powder is favoured by some owners, as this helps to keep the ears dry.

NAIL CLIPPING

How frequently the nails will need to be clipped will depend on

thoroughly shampooed, he requires an equally thorough rinsing. Shampoo left in the coat can be irritating to the dog's skin.

how much a dog walks on hard surfaces, but they should be checked regularly, especially the dewclaws. Under no circumstances should they be allowed to grow so long that they curl under and penetrate the flesh.

Your Pyrenean Mountain Dog should be accustomed to having his nails trimmed at an early age since nail clipping will be part of your maintenance routine throughout his life. Not only does it look nicer, but long nails can scratch someone unintentionally. Also, a long nail has a better chance of ripping and bleeding, or causing the feet to spread. A good rule of thumb is that if you can hear your dog's nails clicking on the floor when he walks, his nails are too long.

Before you start cutting, make sure you can identify the 'quick' in each nail. The quick is a blood vessel that runs through the centre of each nail and grows rather close to the end. The quick will bleed if accidentally cut, which will be quite painful for the dog as it contains nerve endings. Keep some type of clotting agent on hand, such as a styptic pencil or styptic powder (the type used for shaving). This will stop the bleeding quickly when applied to the end of the cut nail. Do not panic if you cut the quick, just stop the bleeding and talk soothingly to your dog. Once he has calmed down, move on to the

The slicker bursh is ideal from removing debris from the Pyrenean's thick coat.

Use a bristle with nylon brush to help remove loose hairs, especially during the moulting season.

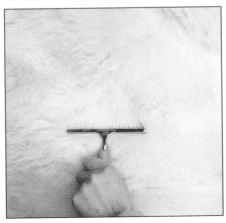

The grooming rake helps to manage the undercoat.

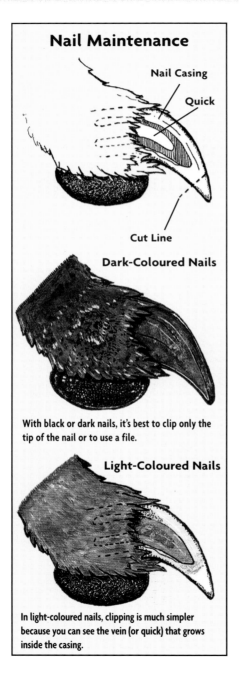

Nail Maintenance

Nail Casing

Quick

Cut Line

Dark-Coloured Nails

With black or dark nails, it's best to clip only the tip of the nail or to use a file.

Light-Coloured Nails

In light-coloured nails, clipping is much simpler because you can see the vein (or quick) that grows inside the casing.

next nail. It is better to clip a little at a time, particularly with black-nailed dogs.

Hold your pup steady as you begin trimming his nails; you do not want him to make any sudden movements or run away. Talk to him soothingly and stroke him as you clip. Holding his foot in your hand, simply take off the end of each nail with one swift clip. You should purchase nail clippers that are made for use on dogs; you can probably find them wherever you buy pet or grooming supplies. Many owners find those of the 'guillotine' design easier to use.

TEETH
Teeth should always be kept as free from tartar as possible. There are now several canine tooth-cleaning agents available, including doggie toothbrushes and canine toothpaste.

CLIPPING THE QUICK
If your Pyrenean Mountain Dog tears its claw, nail polish (of the most simple kind, of course) is a quick sealant. This helps stem the flow of blood and acts as a preventative against dirt getting into the wound. It is important to keep the foot dry and as clean as possible. The homeopathic puncture wound remedy, Hypericum 1M/Ledum 200c, is also worth a try.

TRAVELLING WITH YOUR DOG

CAR TRAVEL

You should accustom your Pyrenean Mountain Dog to riding in a car at an early age. You may or may not take him in the car often, but at the very least he will need to go to the vet and you do not want these trips to be traumatic for the dog or troublesome for you. The safest way for a dog to ride in the car is in his crate.

Put the pup in the crate and see how he reacts. If he seems uneasy, you can have a passenger hold him on his lap while you drive. If you do not have a vehicle that can accommodate the giant crate, another option for car travel is a specially made safety harness for dogs, which straps the dog in much like a seat belt. Do not let the dog roam loose in the vehicle—this is very dangerous! If you should stop short, your dog can be thrown and injured. It is an unsafe situation for everyone—human and canine.

For long trips, be prepared to stop to let the dog relieve himself. Take with you whatever you need to clean up after him, including some paper kitchen towels and perhaps some old towelling for use should he have a toileting accident in the car or suffer from travel sickness.

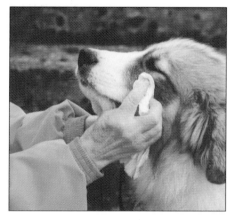

Tear stains can be removed with special cleansers available from your pet shop.

Your dog's ears should be cleaned on a regular basis with an ear-cleaning solution and a soft cotton wipe.

Keep an eye on your pup's growing teeth. Report any abnormalities to your vet.

Acclimate your puppy to travelling in the car, though it's not necessary to give up the front seat. If possible, use your pup's crate for travel, otherwise invest in an harness or safety gate.

AIR TRAVEL

While it is possible to take a dog on a flight within Britain, this is fairly unusual and advance permission is always required. The dog will be required to travel in a fibreglass crate and you should always check in advance with the airline regarding specific requirements. To help put the dog at ease, give him one of his favourite toys in the crate. Do not feed the dog for at least six hours before the trip in order to minimise his need to relieve himself. However, certain regulations specify that water must always be made available to the dog in the crate.

Make sure your dog is properly identified and that your contact information appears on his ID tags and on his crate. Animals travel in a different area of the plane than human passengers, so every rule must be strictly followed so as to prevent the risk of getting separated from your dog.

HOMESITTING

Another option for the travelling dog owner is the homesitter. These unique organisations are comprised of bonded individuals who will stay at your home to look after your pet and property while you are away. Currently these homesitters can be found throughout the UK and are a most convenient option. If the sitter is bonded, owners may receive a reduced insurance premium benefit.

HOLIDAYS AND BOARDING

So you want to take a family holiday—and you want to include *all* members of the family. You would probably make arrangements for accommodation ahead of time anyway, but this is especially important when travelling with a dog. You do not want to make an overnight stop at the only place around for miles, only to find out that they do not allow dogs. Also, you do not want to reserve a place for your family without confirming that you are travelling with a dog, because, if it is against their policy, you may end up without a place to stay.

Alternatively, if you are travelling and choose not to bring your Pyrenean Mountain Dog, you will have to make arrangements for him while you are away. Some options are to take him to a neighbour's house to stay while you are gone, to have a trusted neighbour pop in often or stay at your house or to bring your dog to a reputable boarding kennel. If you choose to board him at a kennel, you should visit in advance to see the facilities provided and where the dogs are kept. Are the dogs' areas spacious enough for a Pyrenean and kept clean? Talk to some of the employees and observe how they treat the dogs—do they spend time with the dogs, play with them, exercise them, etc.? Also find out the kennel's policy on vaccinations and what they require. This is for all of the dogs' safety, since there is a greater risk of diseases being passed from dog to dog when dogs are kept together.

IDENTIFICATION

Your Pyrenean Mountain Dog is your valued companion and friend. That is why you always keep a close eye on him and you have made sure that he cannot escape from the garden or wriggle out of his collar and run away from you. However, accidents can happen and there may come a time when your dog unexpectedly becomes separated from you. If this unfortunate event should occur, the first thing on your mind will be finding him. Proper identification, including an ID tag, a tattoo and possibly a microchip, will increase the chances of his being returned to you safely and quickly.

Every dog should have a light collar to which an ID tag is securely attached.

Training Your
PYRENEAN MOUNTAIN DOG

Living with an untrained dog is a lot like owning a piano that you do not know how to play—it is a nice object to look at but it does not do much more than that to bring you pleasure. Now try taking piano lessons, and suddenly the piano comes alive and brings forth magical sounds and rhythms that set your heart singing and your body swaying.

The same is true with your Pyrenean Mountain Dog. Any dog is a big responsibility and, if not trained sensibly, may develop unacceptable behaviour that annoys you or could even cause family friction.

To train your Pyrenean Mountain Dog, you may like to enrol in an obedience class. Teach your dog good manners as you learn how and why he behaves the way he does. Find out how to communicate with your dog and how to recognise and understand his communications with you. Suddenly the dog takes on a new role in your life—he is clever,

interesting, well behaved and fun to be with. He demonstrates his bond of devotion to you daily. In other words, your Pyrenean does wonders for your ego because he constantly reminds you that you are not only his leader, you are his hero!

Those involved with teaching dog obedience and counselling owners about their dogs' behaviour have discovered some interesting facts about dog ownership. For example, training dogs when they are puppies results in the highest rate of success in developing well-mannered and well-adjusted adult dogs. Training an older dog, from

Positive reinforcement is the basis of most training strategies. Keep your puppy's attention and encourage him for every good thing, and you will have an amenable, enthusiastic student.

Facing page: Pyreneans are interactive, super-intelligent dogs that respond to considerate training methods. Never treat a Pyrenean harshly.

capability and is willing to work patiently to help the dog succeed at developing to his fullest potential. Unfortunately, many owners of untrained adult dogs lack the patience factor, so they do not persist until their dogs are successful at learning particular behaviours.

Training a puppy aged 10 to 16 weeks (20 weeks at the most) is like working with a dry sponge in a pool of water. The pup soaks up whatever you show him and constantly looks for more things to do and learn. At this early age, his body is not yet producing hormones, and therein lies the reason for such a high rate of success. Without hormones, he is focused on his owners and not particularly interested in investigating other places, dogs, people, etc. You are his leader: his provider of food, water, shelter and security. He latches onto you and wants to stay close. He will usually follow you from room to room, will not let you out of his sight when you are outdoors with him and will respond in like manner to the people and animals you encounter. If you greet a friend warmly, he will be happy to greet the person as well. If, however, you are hesitant or anxious about the approach of a stranger, he will respond accordingly.

Once the puppy begins to

REAP THE REWARDS

If you start with a normal, healthy dog and give him time, patience and some carefully executed lessons, you will reap the rewards of that training for the life of the dog. And what a life it will be! The two of you will find immeasurable pleasure in the companionship you have built together with love, respect and understanding.

six months to six years of age, can produce almost equal results providing that the owner accepts the dog's slower rate of learning

PARENTAL GUIDANCE

Training a dog is a life experience. Many parents admit that much of what they know about raising children they learned from caring for their dogs. Dogs respond to love, fairness and guidance, just as children do. Become a good dog owner and you may become an even better parent.

produce hormones, his natural curiosity emerges and he begins to investigate the world around him. It is at this time when you may notice that the untrained dog begins to wander away from you and even ignore your commands to stay close. When this behaviour becomes a problem, you have two choices: get rid of the dog or train him. It is strongly urged that you choose the latter option.

You usually will be able to find obedience classes within a reasonable distance from your home, but you can also do a lot to train your dog yourself. Sometimes there are classes available, but the tuition is too costly. Whatever the circum-stances, the solution to training your dog without obedience classes lies within the pages of this book.

This chapter is devoted to helping you train your Pyrenean Mountain Dog at home. If the

recommended procedures are followed faithfully, you may expect positive results that will prove rewarding both to you and your dog.

Whether your new charge is a puppy or a mature adult, the methods of teaching and the techniques we use in training basic behaviours are the same. After all, no dog, whether puppy or adult, likes harsh or inhumane methods. All creatures, however, respond favourably to gentle motivational methods and sincere praise and encouragement. Now let us get started.

HOUSE-TRAINING

You can train a puppy to relieve himself wherever you choose, but this must be somewhere suitable. You should bear in mind from the outset that when your puppy is old enough to go out in public places, any canine deposits must

A six-week-old Pyrenean puppy will be glued to your every word, though a little tasty titbit doesn't hurt either!

be removed at once. You will always have to carry with you a small plastic bag or 'poop-scoop.'

Outdoor training includes such surfaces as grass, gravel and cement. Indoor training usually means training your dog to newspaper, which is never ideal for a Mountain Dog who can leave mountains and rivers to clean up. When deciding on the surface and

Lead training and house-training go hand in hand. You can practise lead training on the way to the pup's outdoor relief area.

THINK BEFORE YOU BARK

Dogs are sensitive to their masters' moods and emotions. Use your voice wisely when communicating with your dog. Never raise your voice at your dog unless you are angry and trying to correct him. 'Barking' at your dog can become as meaningless as 'dogspeak' is to you. Think before you bark!

you will use each and every time you want your puppy to void. 'Hurry up' and 'Toilet' are examples of commands commonly used by dog owners. Get in the habit of giving the puppy your chosen relief command before you take him out. That way, when he becomes an adult, you will be able to determine if he wants to go out when you ask him. A confirmation will be signs of interest,

location that you will want your Pyrenean to use, be sure it is going to be permanent. Training your dog to grass and then changing your mind a few months later is extremely difficult for both dog and owner.

Next, choose the command

MEALTIME

Mealtime should be a peaceful time for your puppy. Do not put his food and water bowls in a high-traffic area in the house. For example, give him his own little corner of the kitchen where he can eat undisturbed and where he will not be underfoot. Do not allow small children or other family members to disturb the pup when he is eating.

House-training revolves around predicting where the puppy will piddle! You must attach more than a wee importance to your puppy's needs!

wagging his tail, watching you intently, going to the door, etc.

PUPPY'S NEEDS

Puppy needs to relieve himself after play periods, after each meal, after he has been sleeping and at any time he indicates that he is looking for a place to urinate or defecate. The urinary and intestinal tract muscles of very young puppies are not fully developed. Therefore, like human babies, puppies need to relieve themselves frequently.

Take your puppy out often— every hour for an eight-week-old, for example—and always immediately after sleeping and eating. The older the puppy, the less often he will need to relieve himself. Finally, as a mature healthy adult, he will require only three to five relief trips per day.

HOUSING

Since the types of housing and control you provide for your puppy have a direct relationship on the success of house-training, we consider the various aspects of both before we begin training.

Taking a new puppy home and turning him loose in your house can be compared to turning a child loose in a sports arena and telling the child that the place is all his! The sheer enormity of the place would be too much for him to handle. Instead, offer the puppy clearly defined areas where he can play, sleep, eat and live. A room of the house where the family gathers is the most obvious choice. Puppies are social animals and need to feel a part of the pack right from the start. Hearing your voice, watching you while you are doing things and smelling you nearby are all positive reinforcers that he is now a member of your pack. Usually a family room, the kitchen or a nearby adjoining breakfast area is ideal for providing safety and security for both puppy and owner.

HONOUR AND OBEY

Dogs are the most honourable animals in existence. They consider another species (humans) as their own. They interface with you. You are their leader. Puppies perceive children to be on their level; their actions around small children are different from their behaviour around their adult masters.

Within the designated room, there should be a smaller area that the puppy can call his own. An alcove, a wire or fibreglass dog crate or a fenced (not boarded!) corner from which he can view the activities of his new family will be fine. The size of the area or crate is the key factor here. The area must be large enough so that the puppy can lie down and stretch out, as well as stand up, without rubbing his head on the top. At the same time, it must be small enough so that he cannot relieve himself at one end and sleep at the other without coming into contact with his droppings before he is fully trained to relieve himself outside. Dogs are, by nature, clean animals and will not remain close to their relief areas unless forced to do so. In those cases, they then become dirty dogs and usually remain that way for life.

The dog's designated area should contain clean bedding and a toy. Water must always be available, in a non-spill container.

CONTROL

By control, we mean helping the puppy to create a lifestyle pattern that will be compatible to that of his human pack (YOU!). Just as we guide little children to learn our way of life, we must show the puppy when it is time to play, eat, sleep, exercise and even entertain himself.

CANINE DEVELOPMENT SCHEDULE

It is important to understand how and at what age a puppy develops into adulthood.
If you are a puppy owner, consult the following Canine Development Schedule to
determine the stage of development your puppy is currently experiencing.
This knowledge will help you as you work with the puppy in the weeks and months ahead.

Period	Age	Characteristics
FIRST TO THIRD	**BIRTH TO SEVEN WEEKS**	Puppy needs food, sleep and warmth, and responds to simple and gentle touching. Needs mother for security and disciplining. Needs littermates for learning and interacting with other dogs. Pup learns to function within a pack and learns pack order of dominance. Begin socialising with adults and children for short periods. Begins to become aware of its environment.
FOURTH	**EIGHT TO TWELVE WEEKS**	Brain is fully developed. Needs socialising with outside world. Remove from mother and littermates. Needs to change from canine pack to human pack. Human dominance necessary. Fear period occurs between 8 and 12 weeks. Avoid fright and pain.
FIFTH	**THIRTEEN TO SIXTEEN WEEKS**	Training and formal obedience should begin. Less association with other dogs, more with people, places, situations. Period will pass easily if you remember this is pup's change-to-adolescence time. Be firm and fair. Flight instinct prominent. Permissiveness and over-disciplining can do permanent damage. Praise for good behaviour.
JUVENILE	**FOUR TO EIGHT MONTHS**	Another fear period about 7 to 8 months of age. It passes quickly, but be cautious of fright and pain. Sexual maturity reached. Dominant traits established. Dog should understand sit, down, come and stay by now.

NOTE: THESE ARE APPROXIMATE TIME FRAMES. ALLOW FOR INDIVIDUAL DIFFERENCES IN PUPPIES.

play by himself in relative safety and comfort in his designated area. Each time you leave the puppy alone, he should understand exactly where he is to stay.

Puppies are chewers. They cannot tell the difference between lamp cords, television wires, shoes, table legs, etc. Chewing into a television wire, for example, can be fatal to the puppy, while a shorted wire can start a fire in the house. If the puppy chews on the arm of the chair when he is alone, you will probably discipline him angrily when you get home. Thus, he makes the association that your coming home means he is going to be punished. (He will not remember chewing the chair and is incapable of making the associ-ation of the discipline with his naughty deed.) Accustoming the pup to his designated area not only keeps him safe but also avoids his engaging in destructive behaviours when you are not around.

Times of excitement, such as special occasions, family parties, etc., can be fun for the puppy providing that he can view the activities from the security of his designated area. He is not underfoot and he is not being fed all sorts of titbits that will probably cause him stomach distress, yet he still feels a part of the fun.

TAKE THE LEAD
Do not carry your dog to his toilet area. Lead him there on a leash or, better yet, encourage him to follow you to the spot. If you start carrying him to his spot, you might end up doing this routine forever and your dog will have the satisfaction of having trained YOU.

Your puppy should always sleep in his crate. He should also learn that, during times of household confusion and excessive human activity, such as at breakfast when family members are preparing for the day, he can

SCHEDULE

A puppy should be taken to his relief area each time he is released from his designated area, after meals, after a play session and when he first awakens in the morning (at age eight weeks, this can mean 5 a.m.!). The puppy will indicate that he's ready 'to go' by circling or sniffing busily—do not misinterpret these signs. For a puppy less than ten weeks of age, a routine of taking him out every hour is necessary. As the puppy grows, he will be able to wait for longer periods of time.

Keep trips to his relief area short. Stay no more than five or six minutes and then return to the house. If he goes during that time, praise him lavishly and take him indoors immediately. If he does not, but he has an accident when you go back indoors, pick him up immediately, say 'No! No!' and return to his relief area. Wait a few minutes, then return to the house again. Never hit a puppy or rub his face in urine or excrement when he has had an accident!

Once indoors, put the puppy in his crate until you have had time to clean up his accident. Then, release him to the family area and watch him more closely than before. Chances are, his accident was a result of your not picking up his signal or waiting too long before offering him the opportunity to relieve himself. Never hold a grudge against the puppy for accidents.

Let the puppy learn that going outdoors means it is time to relieve himself, not to play. Once trained, he will be able to play indoors and out and still differentiate between the times for play

HOW MANY TIMES A DAY?

AGE	RELIEF TRIPS
To 14 weeks	10
14–22 weeks	8
22–32 weeks	6
Adulthood	4
(dog stops growing)	

These are estimates, of course, but they are a guide to the MINIMUM opportunities a dog should have each day to relieve himself.

versus the times for relief.

Help him develop regular hours for naps, being alone, playing by himself and just resting, all in his crate. Encourage him to entertain himself while you are busy with your activities. Let him learn that having you near is comforting, but it is not your main purpose in life to provide him with undivided attention.

Each time you put your puppy in his own area, use the same command, whatever suits best. Soon he will run to his crate or special area when he hears you say those words.

Crate training provides safety for you, the puppy and the home. It also provides the puppy with a feeling of security, and that helps the puppy achieve self-confidence and clean habits. Remember that

THE SUCCESS METHOD

6 Steps to Successful Crate Training

1 Tell the puppy 'Crate time!' and place him in the crate with a small treat (a piece of cheese or half of a biscuit). Let him stay in the crate for five minutes while you are in the same room. Then release him and praise lavishly. Never release him when he is fussing. Wait until he is quiet before you let him out.

2 Repeat Step 1 several times a day.

3 The next day, place the puppy in the crate as before. Let him stay there for ten minutes. Do this several times.

4 Continue building time in five-minute increments until the puppy stays in his crate for 30 minutes with you in the room. Always take him to his relief area after prolonged periods in his crate.

5 Now go back to Step 1 and let the puppy stay in his crate for five minutes, this time while you are out of the room.

6 Once again, build crate time in five-minute increments with you out of the room. When the puppy will stay willingly in his crate (he may even fall asleep!) for 30 minutes with you out of the room, he will be ready to stay in it for several hours at a time.

KEY TO SUCCESS
Success that comes by luck is usually short-lived. Success that comes by well-thought-out proven methods is often more easily achieved and permanent. This is the Success Method. It is designed to give you, the puppy owner, a simple yet proven way to help your puppy develop clean living habits and a feeling of security in his new environment.

following these procedures with a normal, healthy puppy, you and the puppy will soon be past the stage of 'accidents' and ready to move on to a full and rewarding life together.

ROLES OF DISCIPLINE, REWARD AND PUNISHMENT

Discipline, training one to act in accordance with rules, brings order to life. It is as simple as that. Without discipline, particularly in a group society, chaos will

one of the primary ingredients in house-training your puppy is control. Regardless of your lifestyle, there will always be occasions when you will need to have a place where your dog can stay and be happy and safe. Crate training is the answer for now and in the future.

In conclusion, a few key elements are really all you need for a successful house-training method—consistency, frequency, praise, control and supervision. By

Always clean up after your dog, whether you are in a public place or your own garden.

reign supreme and the group will eventually perish. Humans and canines are social animals and need some form of discipline in order to function effectively. They must procure food, protect their home base and their young and reproduce to keep their species going. If there were no discipline in the lives of social animals, they would eventually die from starvation and/or predation by other stronger animals.

OPEN MINDS
Dogs are as different from each other as people are. What works for one dog may not work for another. Have an open mind. If one method of training is unsuccessful, try another.

TRAINING TIP
Dogs will do anything for your attention. If you reward the dog when he is calm and resting, you will develop a well-mannered dog. If, on the other hand, you greet your dog excitedly and encourage him to wrestle with you, the dog will greet you the same way and you will have a hyperactive dog on your hands.

In the case of domestic canines, discipline in their lives is needed in order for them to understand how their pack (you and other family members) functions and how they must act in order to survive.

A large humane society in a highly populated area recently surveyed dog owners regarding their satisfaction with their relationships with their dogs. People who had trained their dogs were 75% more satisfied with their pets than those who had never trained their dogs.

Dr Edward Thorndike, a psychologist, established *Thorndike's Theory of Learning*, which states that a behaviour that results in a pleasant event tends to be repeated and, conversely, a behaviour that results in an unpleasant event tends not to be repeated. It is this theory

THE GOLDEN RULE
The golden rule of dog training is simple. For each 'question' (command), there is only one correct answer (reaction). One command = one reaction. Keep practising the command until the dog reacts correctly without hesitating. Be repetitive but not monotonous. Dogs get bored just as people do!

upon which training methods are based today. For example, if you coax a dog to perform a specific behaviour and reward him for doing it, he is likely to do it again because he enjoyed the end result.

Occasionally, punishment, a penalty inflicted for an offence, is necessary. The best type of punishment often comes from an outside source. For example, a child is told not to touch the stove because he may get burned. He disobeys and touches the stove. In doing so, he receives a burn. From that time on, he respects the heat of the stove and avoids contact with it. Therefore, a behaviour that results in an unpleasant event tends not to be repeated.

PRACTICE MAKES PERFECT!

• Have training lessons with your dog every day in several short segments— three to five times a day for a few minutes at a time is ideal.
• Do not have long practice sessions. The dog will become easily bored.
• Never practise when you are tired, ill, worried or in an otherwise negative mood. This will transmit to the dog and may have an adverse effect on its performance.

Think fun, short and above all POSITIVE! End each session on a high note, rather than a failed exercise, and make sure to give a lot of praise. Enjoy the training and help your dog enjoy it, too.

A good example of a dog learning the hard way is the dog who chases the house cat. He is told many times to leave the cat alone, yet he persists in teasing the cat. Then, one day, the dog begins chasing the cat but the cat turns and swipes a claw across the dog's face, leaving the dog with a painful gash on his nose. The final result is that the dog stops chasing the cat. Again, a behaviour that results in an unpleasant event tends not to be repeated.

Breeders spend time interacting with, handling and teaching good manners to the baby puppies so that they will be well adjusted and amenable to training in their new homes.

TRAINING EQUIPMENT

COLLAR AND LEAD

For a Pyrenean Mountain Dog, the collar and lead that you use for training must be one with which you are easily able to work, not too light or heavy for the dog and perfectly safe.

TREATS

Have a bag of treats on hand; something nutritious and easy to swallow works best. Use a soft treat, a chunk of cheese or a piece of cooked chicken rather than a dry biscuit. By the time the dog has finished chewing a dry treat, he will forget why he is being rewarded in the first place!

Using food rewards will not teach a dog to beg at the table— the only way to teach a dog to beg at the table is to give him food from the table. In training, rewarding the dog with a food treat will help him associate praise and the treats with learning new behaviours that obviously please his owner.

TRAINING BEGINS: ASK THE DOG A QUESTION

In order to teach your dog anything, you must first get his attention. After all, he cannot learn anything if he is looking away from you with his mind on something else.

To get your dog's attention, ask him 'School?', and immediately walk over to him and give him a treat as you tell him 'Good dog.' Wait a minute or two and repeat the routine, this time with a treat in your hand as you approach within a foot of the dog. Do not go directly to him, but stop about a foot short of him and hold out the treat as you ask 'School?' He will see you approaching with

a treat in your hand and most likely begin walking toward you. As you meet, give him the treat and praise again.

The third time, ask the question, have a treat in your hand and walk only a short distance toward the dog so that he must walk almost all the way to you. As he reaches you, give him the treat and praise again.

By this time, the dog will probably be getting the idea that if he pays attention to you, especially when you ask that question, it will pay off in treats and enjoyable activities for him. In other words, he learns that 'school' means doing great things with you that are fun and that result in positive attention for him.

Remember that the dog does not understand your verbal language; he only recognises sounds. Your question translates to a series of sounds for him, and those sounds become the signal to go to you and pay attention. The dog learns that if he does this, he will get to interact with you plus receive treats and praise.

THE BASIC COMMANDS

TEACHING SIT

Now that you have the dog's attention, attach his lead and hold it in your left hand, and hold a food treat in your right hand. Place your food hand at the dog's nose and let him lick the treat but not take it from you. Say 'Sit' and slowly raise your food hand from in front of the dog's nose up over his head so that he is looking at the ceiling. As he bends his head upward, he will have to bend his knees to maintain his balance. As he bends his knees, he will assume a sit position. At that point, release the food treat and praise lavishly with comments such as 'Good dog! Good sit!,' etc. Remember to always praise enthusiastically, because dogs relish verbal praise from their owners and feel so proud of themselves whenever they accomplish a behaviour.

You will not use food forever in getting the dog to obey your commands. Food is only used to teach new behaviours and, once the dog knows what you want when you give a specific command, you will wean him off the food treats but still maintain the verbal praise. After all, you will always have your voice with you, and there will be many times when you have no food rewards but expect the dog to obey.

TEACHING DOWN

Teaching the down exercise is easy when you understand how the dog perceives the down position, and it is very difficult when you do not. Dogs perceive

Training a dog to sit requires both verbal communication (teaching to dog to recognise the sound of the word 'sit') as well as physical contact so that the dog understands what is expected of him.

the down position as a submissive one; therefore, teaching the down exercise by using a forceful method can sometimes make the dog develop such a fear of the down that he either runs away when you say 'Down' or he attempts to snap at the person who tries to force him down.

Have the dog sit close alongside your left leg, facing in the same direction as you are. Hold the lead in your left hand and a food treat in your right. Now place your left hand lightly on the top of the dog's shoulders where they meet above the spinal cord. Do not push down on the dog's shoulders; simply rest your

Food and praise are key to teaching the Pyrenean puppy to sit/stay. Be patient and positive and your Pyr will respond in due course.

> ## DOUBLE JEOPARDY
> A dog in jeopardy never lies down. He stays alert on his feet because instinct tells him that he may have to run away or fight for his survival. Therefore, if a dog feels threatened or anxious, he will not lie down. Consequently, it is important to have the dog calm and relaxed as he learns the down exercise.

left hand there so you can guide the dog to lie down close to your left leg rather than to swing away from your side when he drops.

Now place the food hand at the dog's nose, say 'Down' very softly (almost a whisper), and slowly lower the food hand to the dog's front feet. When the food hand reaches the floor, begin moving it forward along the floor in front of the dog. Keep talking softly to the dog, saying things like, 'Do you want this treat? You can do this, good dog.' Your reassuring tone of voice will help calm the dog as he tries to follow the food hand in order to get the treat.

When the dog's elbows touch the floor, release the food and praise softly. Try to get the dog to maintain that down position for several seconds before you let him sit up again. The goal here is to get the dog to settle down and not feel threatened in the down position.

TEACHING STAY

It is easy to teach the dog to stay in either a sit or a down position. Again, we use food and praise

FEAR AGGRESSION

Pups who are subjected to physical abuse during training commonly end up with behavioural problems as adults. One common result of abuse is fear aggression, in which a dog will lash out, bare his teeth, snarl and finally bite someone by whom he feels threatened. For example, your daughter may be playing with the dog one afternoon. As they play hide-and-seek, she backs the dog into a corner and, as she attempts to tease him playfully, he bites her hand. Examine the cause of this behaviour. Did your daughter ever hit the dog? Did someone who resembles your daughter hit or scream at the dog?

Fortunately, fear aggression is relatively easy to correct. Have your daughter engage in only positive activities with the dog, such as feeding, petting and walking. She should not give any corrections or negative feedback. If the dog still growls or cowers away from her, allow someone else to accompany them. After approximately one week, the dog should feel that he can rely on her for many positive things, and he will also be prevented from reacting fearfully towards anyone who might resemble her.

during the teaching process as we help the dog to understand exactly what it is that we are expecting him to do.

To teach the sit/stay, start with the dog sitting on your left side as before and hold the lead in your left hand. Have a food treat in your right hand and place your food hand at the dog's nose. Say 'Stay' and step out on your right foot to stand directly in front of the dog, toe to toe, as he licks and nibbles the treat. Be sure to keep his head facing upward to maintain the sit position. Count to five and then swing around to stand next to the dog again with him on your left. As soon as you get back to the original position, release the food and praise lavishly.

To teach the down/stay, do the down as previously described. As soon as the dog lies down, say 'Stay' and step out on your right foot just as you did in the sit/stay. Count to five and then return to stand beside the dog with him on your left side. Release the treat and praise as always.

Within a week to ten days, you can begin to add a bit of distance between you and your dog when you leave him. When you do, use your left hand open with the palm facing the dog as a stay signal, much the same as the hand signal a constable uses to stop traffic at an intersection. Hold the food treat in your right

Lead training reinforces the puppy's trust and confidence in you as the leader. Since walking will be a major part of your puppy's house-training procedure, it is helpful to initiate this training before you begin teaching commands.

come when called. The secret, it seems, is never to teach the word 'come.'

At times when an owner most wants his dog to come when called, the owner is likely to be upset or anxious and he allows these feelings to come through in the tone of his voice when he calls his dog. Hearing that desperation in his owner's voice, the dog fears the results of going to him and therefore either disobeys outright or runs in the opposite direction. The secret, therefore, is to teach the dog a game and, when you want him to come to you, simply play the game. It is practically a no-fail solution!

To begin, have several members of your family take a few food treats and each go into a different room in the house.

hand as before, but this time the food will not be touching the dog's nose. He will watch the food hand and quickly learn that he is going to get that treat as soon as you return to his side.

When you can stand 1 metre away from your dog for 30 seconds, you can then begin building time and distance in both stays. Eventually, the dog can be expected to remain in the stay position for prolonged periods of time until you return to him or call him to you. Always praise lavishly when he stays.

TEACHING COME

If you make teaching 'come' an exciting experience, you should never have a 'student' that does not love the game or that fails to

CONSISTENCY PAYS OFF

Dogs need consistency in their feeding schedule, exercise and toilet breaks, and in the verbal commands you use. If you use 'Stay' on Monday and 'Stay here, please' on Tuesday, you will confuse your dog. Don't demand perfect behaviour during training classes and then let him have the run of the house the rest of the day. Above all, lavish praise on your pet consistently every time he does something right. The more he feels he is pleasing you, the more willing he will be to learn.

Everyone takes turns calling the dog, and each person should celebrate the dog's finding him with a treat and lots of happy praise. When a person calls the dog, he is actually inviting the dog to find him and to get a treat as a reward for 'winning.'

A few turns of the 'Where are you?' game and the dog will understand that everyone is playing the game and that each person has a big celebration awaiting the dog's success at locating him or her. Once the dog learns to love the game, simply calling out 'Where are you?' will bring him running from wherever he is when he hears that all-important question.

The come command is recognised as one of the most important things to teach a dog, but there are trainers who work with thousands of dogs and never teach the actual word 'Come.' Yet these dogs will race to respond to a person who uses the dog's name followed by 'Where are you?' For

Heel training follows lead training, requiring that the puppy not only accept the lead but walk in an acceptable manner at the owner's side.

example, a woman has a 10-year-old companion dog who went blind, but who never fails to locate her owner when asked, 'Where are you?'

Children, in particular, love to play this game with their dogs. Children can hide in smaller places like a shower or bath, behind a bed or under a table. The dog needs to work a little bit harder to find these hiding places, but, when he does, he loves to celebrate with a treat and a tussle with a favourite youngster.

TEACHING HEEL

Heeling means that the dog walks beside the owner without pulling. It takes time and patience on the owner's part to succeed at teaching the dog that he (the owner) will not proceed unless the dog is walking calmly beside him. Neither pulling out ahead on the lead nor lagging behind is

acceptable. Begin heel training as young as possible, as it will be nearly impossible to train on unruly adult Pyrenean.

Begin by holding the lead in your left hand as the dog sits beside your left leg. Move the loop end of the lead to your right hand, but keep your left hand short on the lead so that it keeps the dog in close next to you.

Say 'Heel' and step forward on your left foot. Keep the dog close to you and take three steps. Stop and have the dog sit next to you in what we now call the 'heel position.' Praise verbally, but do not touch the dog. Hesitate a moment and begin again with 'Heel,' taking three steps and stopping, at which point the dog is told to sit again.

Your goal here is to have the dog walk those three steps without pulling on the lead. Once he will walk calmly beside you for three steps without pulling, increase the number of steps you take to five. When he will walk politely beside you while you take five steps, you can increase the length of your walk to ten steps. Keep increasing the length of your stroll until the dog will walk quietly beside you without pulling as long as you want him to heel. When you stop heeling, indicate to the dog that the exercise is over by verbally praising as you pet him and say, 'OK, good dog.' The 'OK' is used

longer distances. Remember also to give the dog free time and the opportunity to run and play when you have finished heel practice.

WEANING OFF FOOD IN TRAINING

Food is used in training new behaviours. Once the dog understands what behaviour goes with a specific command, it is time to start weaning him off the food treats. At first, give a treat after each exercise. Then, start to give a treat only after every other exercise. Vary the times when you offer a food reward and the times when you only offer praise so that

as a release word, meaning that the exercise is finished and the dog is free to relax.

If you are dealing with a dog who insists on pulling you around, simply 'put on your brakes' and stand your ground until the dog realises that the two of you are not going anywhere until he is beside you and moving at your pace, not his. It may take some time just standing there to convince the dog that you are the leader and that you will be the one to decide on the direction and speed of your travel.

Each time the dog looks up at you or slows down to give a slack lead between the two of you, quietly praise him and say, 'Good heel. Good dog.' Eventually, the dog will begin to respond and within a few days he will be walking politely beside you without pulling on the lead. At first, the training sessions should be kept short and very positive; soon the dog will be able to walk nicely with you for increasingly

A Pyrenean must be properly heel trained for daily walks as well as for exhibiting in the show ring. Practising the Pyr's gaiting on the end of a loose lead is ideal for promising show dogs.

the dog will never know when he is going to receive both food and praise and when he is going to receive only praise. This is called a variable ratio reward system. It proves successful because there is always the chance that the owner will produce a treat, so the dog never stops trying for that reward. No matter what, *always* give verbal praise.

OBEDIENCE CLASSES

It is a good idea to enrol in an obedience class if one is available in your area. If yours is a show dog, ringcraft classes would be more appropriate. Many areas have dog clubs that offer basic obedience training as well as preparatory classes for obedience competition. There are also local dog trainers who

Keep training sessions brief and interesting. Pyreneans bore more quickly than many breeds.

offer similar classes.

At obedience shows, dogs can earn titles at various levels of competition. The beginning levels of obedience competition include basic behaviours such as sit, down, heel, etc. The more advanced levels of competition include jumping, retrieving, scent discrimination and signal work. The advanced levels require a dog and owner to put a lot of time and effort into their training. The titles that can be earned at these levels of competition are very prestigious.

As an obedience dog, the Pyrenean Mountain Dog is a quick learner, but bores easily once it has learned the basics of an exercise. Lessons should be kept short, and as much fun as possible should be incorporated into them. This breed has little chase or retrieve instinct.

OTHER ACTIVITIES FOR LIFE

Whether a dog is trained in the structured environment of a class or alone with his owner at home, there are many activities that can bring fun and rewards to both owner and dog once they have mastered basic control. For example, the Pyrenean Mountain Dog is still used for its original purpose of guarding livestock.

Teaching the dog to help out around the home, in the garden or on the farm provides great satisfaction to both dog and owner. In addition, the dog's help makes life a little easier for his owner and raises his stature as a valued companion to his family. It helps give the dog a purpose by occupying his mind and providing an outlet for his energy.

Backpacking is an exciting and healthy activity that the dog can be taught without assistance from more than his owner. The exercise of walking and climbing is good for man and dog alike, and the bond that they develop together is priceless. The rule for backpacking with any dog is never to expect the dog to carry more than one-sixth of his body weight.

If you are interested in participating in organised competition with your Pyrenean, there are activities other than obedience in which you and your dog can become involved. Agility is a popular sport in which dogs run through an obstacle course that includes various jumps, tunnels and other exercises to test the dog's speed and coordination. The owners run beside their dogs to give commands and to guide them through the course. Although competitive, the focus is on fun—it's fun to do, fun to watch and great exercise.

PYRENEAN MOUNTAIN DOG

Dogs suffer from many of the same physical illnesses as people. They might even share many of the same psychological problems. Since people usually know more about human diseases than canine maladies, many of the terms used in this chapter will be familiar but not necessarily those used by veterinary surgeons. We will use the term *x-ray*, instead of the more acceptable term *radiograph*. We will also use the familiar term *symptoms* even though dogs don't have symptoms, which are verbal descriptions of the patient's feelings; dogs have *clinical signs*. Since dogs can't speak, we have to look for clinical signs...but we still use the term *symptoms* in this book.

As a general rule, medicine is *practised*. That term is not arbitrary. Medicine is a constantly changing art as we learn more and more about genetics, electronic aids (like CAT scans) and daily laboratory advances. There are many dog maladies, like canine hip dysplasia, which are not universally treated in the same manner. Some veterinary surgeons opt for surgery more often than others do.

SELECTING A VETERINARY SURGEON

Your selection of a veterinary surgeon should not be based upon personality (as most are) but upon his convenience to your home. You want a vet who is close because you might have emergencies or need to make multiple visits for treatments. You want a vet who has services that you might require such as tattooing and grooming, as well as sophisticated pet supplies and a good reputation for ability and responsiveness. There is nothing more frustrating than having to wait a day or more to get a response from your veterinary surgeon.

Recognise the signs of good health on a growing Pyrenean Mountain Dog.

Facing page: The Pyrenean Mountain Dog relies upon his owner for his continued good health. In addition to a balanced diet, exercise and proper care, qualified veterinary attention is a vital component to the dog's well-being.

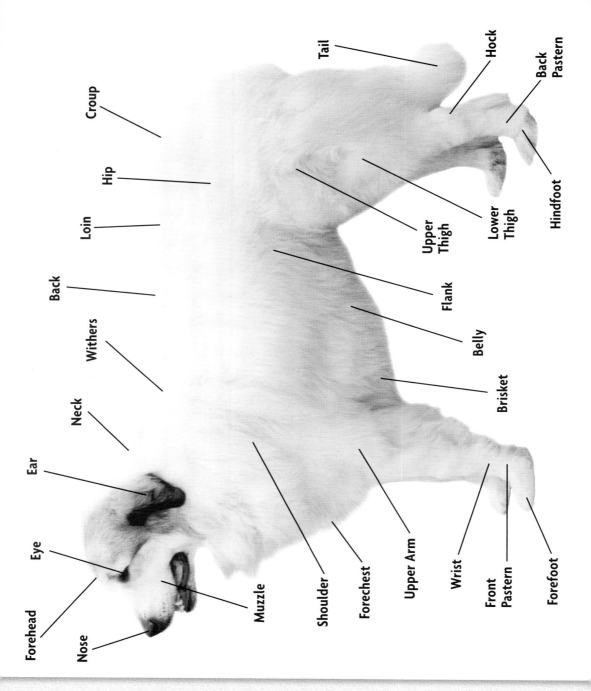

PHYSICAL STRUCTURE OF THE PYRENEAN MOUNTAIN DOG

All veterinary surgeons are licensed and their diplomas and/or certificates should be displayed in their waiting rooms. There are, however, many veterinary specialities that usually require further studies and internships. There are specialists in heart problems (veterinary cardiologists), skin problems (veterinary dermatologists), teeth and gum problems (veterinary dentists), eye problems (veterinary ophthalmologists) and x-rays (veterinary radiologists), as well as vets who have specialities in bones, muscles or other organs. Most veterinary surgeons do routine surgery such as neutering, stitching up wounds and docking tails for those breeds in which such is required for show purposes.

When the problem affecting your dog is serious, it is not unusual or impudent to get another medical opinion, although in Britain you are obliged to advise the vets concerned about this. You might also want to compare costs among several veterinary surgeons. Sophisticated health care and veterinary services can be very costly. It is quite acceptable to discuss matters of cost with your vet; if there is more than one treatment option, cost may be a factor in deciding which route to take.

PREVENTATIVE MEDICINE

It is much easier, less costly and more effective to practise preventative medicine than to fight bouts of illness and disease. Properly bred puppies come from parents who were selected based upon their genetic disease profiles. Their mothers should have been vaccinated, free of all internal and external parasites and properly nourished. The dam can pass on disease resistance to her puppies, which can last for eight to ten weeks, but she can also pass on parasites and many infections. For these reasons, a visit to the veterinary surgeon who cared for the dam is recommended.

VACCINATION SCHEDULING

Most vaccinations are given by injection and should only be done by a veterinary surgeon. Both he and you should keep records of the date of the injection, the identification of the vaccine and the amount given. Some vets give a first vaccination at eight weeks, but most dog breeders prefer the course not to commence until about ten weeks to avoid negating any antibodies passed on by the dam. The vaccination scheduling is usually based on a 15-day cycle. You must take your vet's advice regarding when to vaccinate, as this may differ according to the vaccine used. Most vaccinations immunize your puppy against viruses.

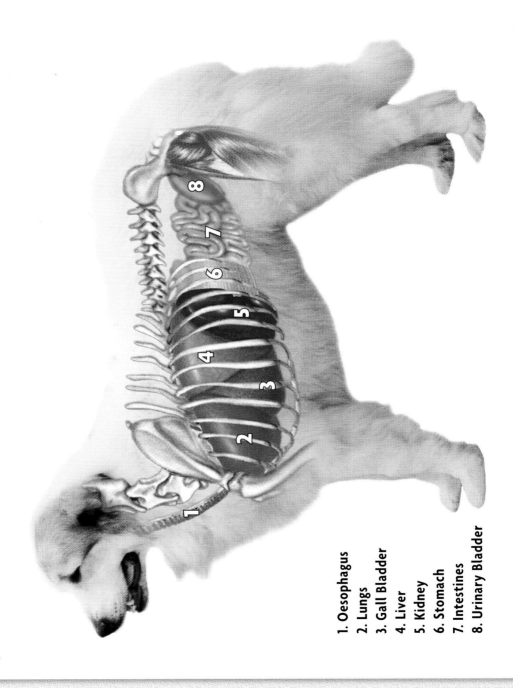

1. Oesophagus
2. Lungs
3. Gall Bladder
4. Liver
5. Kidney
6. Stomach
7. Intestines
8. Urinary Bladder

INTERNAL ORGANS OF THE PYRENEAN MOUNTAIN DOG

The usual vaccines contain immunizing doses of several different viruses such as distemper, parvovirus, parainfluenza and hepatitis, although some veterinary surgeons recommend separate vaccines for each disease. There are other vaccines available when the puppy is at risk. You should rely upon professional advice. This is especially true for the booster-shot programme. Most vaccination programmes require a booster when the puppy is a year old and once a year thereafter. In some cases, circumstances may require more or less frequent immunizations. Kennel cough, more

Breakdown of Veterinary Income by Category

2%	Dentistry
4%	Radiology
12%	Surgery
15%	Vaccinations
19%	Laboratory
23%	Examinations
25%	Medicines

A typical vet's income, categorised according to services performed. This survey dealt with small-animal (pets) practices in the US.

HEALTH AND VACCINATION SCHEDULE

Age in Weeks:	6th	8th	10th	12th	14th	16th	20-24th	1 yr
Worm Control	✔	✔	✔	✔	✔	✔	✔	
Neutering								✔
Heartworm		✔		✔		✔	✔	
Parvovirus	✔		✔		✔		✔	✔
Distemper		✔		✔		✔		✔
Hepatitis		✔		✔		✔		✔
Leptospirosis								✔
Parainfluenza	✔		✔		✔			✔
Dental Examination		✔					✔	✔
Complete Physical		✔					✔	✔
Coronavirus				✔			✔	✔
Kennel Cough	✔							
Hip Dysplasia								✔
Rabies							✔	

Vaccinations are not instantly effective. It takes about two weeks for the dog's immune system to develop antibodies. Most vaccinations require annual booster shots. Your veterinary surgeon should guide you in this regard.

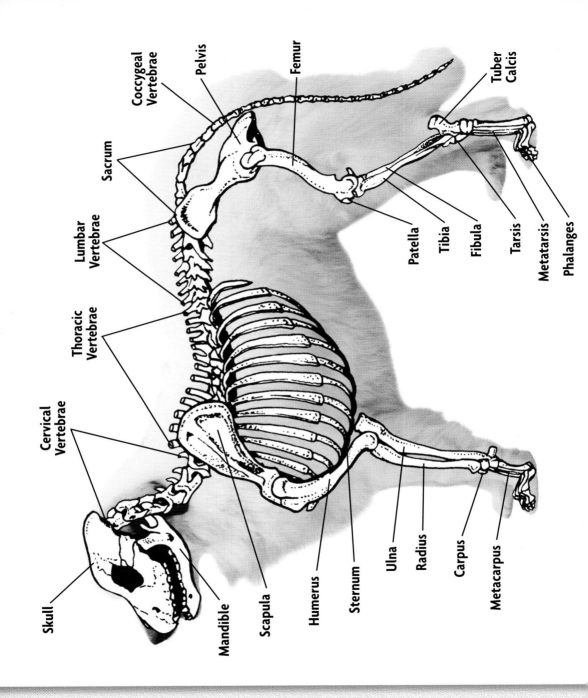

SKELETAL STRUCTURE OF THE PYRENEAN MOUNTAIN DOG

formally known as tracheobron-
chitis, is treated with a vaccine
that is sprayed into the dog's
nostrils. Kennel cough is usually
included in routine vaccination,
but this is often not so effective as
for other major diseases.

WEANING TO FIVE MONTHS OLD

Puppies should be weaned by the
time they are about two months
old. A puppy that remains for at
least eight weeks with its mother
and littermates usually adapts
better to other dogs and people
later in life. Some new owners

have their puppies examined by
veterinary surgeons immediately,
which is a good idea. Vaccination
programmes usually begin when
the puppy is very young.

The puppy will have its teeth
examined and have its skeletal
conformation and general health
checked prior to certification by
the veterinary surgeon. Puppies in
certain breeds may have problems
with their kneecaps, cataracts and
other eye problems, heart
murmurs or undescended
testicles. They may also have
personality problems, and your

DISEASE REFERENCE CHART

	What is it?	What causes it?	Symptoms
Leptospirosis	Severe disease that affects the internal organs; can be spread to people.	A bacterium, which is often carried by rodents, that enters through mucous membranes and spreads quickly throughout the body.	Range from fever, vomiting and loss of appetite in less severe cases to shock, irreversible kidney damage and possibly death in most severe cases.
Rabies	Potentially deadly virus that infects warm-blooded mammals. Not seen in United Kingdom.	Bite from a carrier of the virus, mainly wild animals.	1st stage: dog exhibits change in behaviour, fear. 2nd stage: dog's behaviour becomes more aggressive. 3rd stage: loss of coordination, trouble with bodily functions.
Parvovirus	Highly contagious virus, potentially deadly.	Ingestion of the virus, which is usually spread through the faeces of infected dogs.	Most common: severe diarrhoea. Also vomiting, fatigue, lack of appetite.
Kennel cough	Contagious respiratory infection.	Combination of types of bacteria and virus. Most common: *Bordetella bronchiseptica* bacteria and parainfluenza virus.	Chronic cough.
Distemper	Disease primarily affecting respiratory and nervous system.	Virus that is related to the human measles virus.	Mild symptoms such as fever, lack of appetite and mucous secretion progress to evidence of brain damage, 'hard pad.'
Hepatitis	Virus primarily affecting the liver.	Canine adenovirus type I (CAV-1). Enters system when dog breathes in particles.	Lesser symptoms include listlessness, diarrhoea, vomiting. More severe symptoms include 'blue-eye' (clumps of virus in eye).
Coronavirus	Virus resulting in digestive problems.	Virus is spread through infected dog's faeces.	Stomach upset evidenced by lack of appetite, vomiting, diarrhoea.

  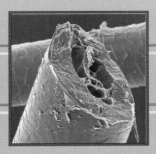

Normal hairs of a dog enlarged 200 times original size. The cuticle (outer covering) is clean and healthy. Unlike human hair that grows from the base, a dog's hair also grows from the end. Damaged hairs and split ends, illustrated above.

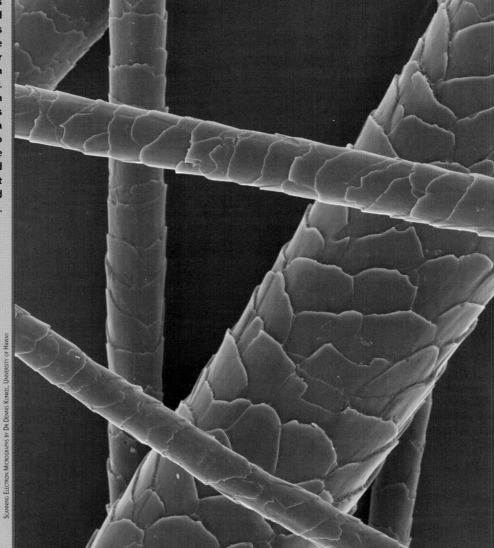

VACCINE ALLERGIES

Vaccines do not work all the time. Sometimes dogs are allergic to them and many times the antibodies, which are supposed to be stimulated by the vaccine, just are not produced. You should keep your dog in the veterinary clinic for an hour after it is vaccinated to be sure there are no allergic reactions.

veterinary surgeon might have training in temperament evaluation.

FIVE TO TWELVE MONTHS OF AGE

Unless you intend to breed or show your dog, neutering the puppy at six months of age is recommended. Discuss this with your veterinary surgeon. Neutering has proven to be extremely beneficial to both male and female puppies. Besides eliminating the possibility of pregnancy, it inhibits (but does not prevent) breast cancer in bitches and prostate cancer in male dogs. Under no circumstances should a bitch be spayed prior to her first season.

Your veterinary surgeon should provide your puppy with a thorough dental evaluation at six months of age, ascertaining whether all the permanent teeth have erupted properly. A home dental care regimen should be initiated at six months, including brushing weekly and providing good dental devices (such as nylon bones). Regular dental care promotes healthy teeth, fresh breath and a longer life.

ONE TO SEVEN YEARS

Once a year, your dog should visit the vet for an examination and vaccination boosters, if needed. Some vets recommend blood tests, a thyroid level check and a dental evaluation to accompany these annual visits. A thorough clinical evaluation by the vet can provide critical background information for your dog. Blood tests are often performed at one year of age, and dental examinations around the third or fourth birthday. In the long run, quality preventative care for your pet can save money, teeth and lives.

SKIN PROBLEMS

Veterinary surgeons are consulted by dog owners for skin problems more than for any other group of diseases or maladies. Dogs' skin is almost as sensitive as human skin, and both suffer from almost the same ailments (though the occurrence of acne in dogs is rare!). For this reason, veterinary dermatology has developed into a speciality practised by many veterinary surgeons.

Since many skin problems have visual symptoms that are almost identical, it requires the skill of an experienced veterinary

BE CAREFUL WHERE YOU WALK YOUR DOG

Dogs who have been exposed to lawns sprayed with herbicides have double and triple the rate of malignant lymphoma. Town dogs are especially at risk, as they are exposed to tailored lawns and gardens. Dogs perspire and absorb through their footpads. Be careful where your dog walks and always avoid any area that appears yellowed from chemical overspray.

disorder, you should seek professional assistance as quickly as possible. As with all diseases, the earlier a problem is identified and treated, the more successful is the cure.

HEREDITARY SKIN DISORDERS

Veterinary dermatologists are currently researching a number of skin disorders that are believed to have an hereditary basis. These inherited diseases are transmitted by both parents, who appear (phenotypically) normal but have a recessive gene for the disease, meaning that they carry, but are not affected by, the disease. These diseases pose serious problems to breeders because in some instances there are no methods of identifying carriers. Often the secondary diseases associated with these skin conditions are even more debilitating than the skin disorders themselves, including cancers and respiratory problems; others can be lethal.

Among the hereditary skin disorders, for which the mode of inheritance is known, are acrodermatitis, cutaneous asthenia (Ehlers-Danlos syndrome), sebaceous adenitis, cyclic hematopoiesis, dermatomyositis, IgA deficiency, colour dilution alopaecia and nodular dermatofibrosis. Some of these disorders are limited to one or two breeds, while others affect a large number of breeds. All inherited diseases

dermatologist to identify and cure many of the more severe skin disorders. Pet shops sell many treatments for skin problems, but most of the treatments are directed at the symptoms and not the underlying problem(s). If your dog is suffering from a skin

must be diagnosed and treated by a veterinary specialist.

PARASITE BITES

Many of us are allergic to insect bites. The bites itch, erupt and may even become infected. Dogs have the same reaction to fleas, ticks and/or mites. When an insect lands on you, you have the chance to whisk it away with your hand. Unfortunately, when your dog is bitten by a flea, tick or mite, he can only scratch it away or bite it. By the time the dog has been bitten, the parasite has done some of its damage. It may also have laid eggs, which will cause further problems in the near future. The itching from parasite bites is probably due to the saliva injected into the site when the parasite sucks the dog's blood.

AUTO-IMMUNE SKIN CONDITIONS

An auto-immune skin condition is commonly referred to as a condition in which a person (or dog) is 'allergic' to him- or herself, while an allergy is usually an inflammatory reaction to an outside stimulus. Auto-immune diseases cause serious damage to the tissues that are involved.

The best known auto-immune disease is lupus, which affects people as well as dogs. The symptoms are variable and may affect the kidneys, bones, blood chemistry and skin. It can be fatal to both dogs and humans, though it is not thought to be transmissible. It is usually successfully treated with cortisone, prednisone or a similar corticosteroid, but extensive use of these drugs can have harmful side effects.

ACRAL LICK GRANULOMA

Many large dogs have a very poorly understood syndrome called acral lick granuloma. The manifestation of the problem is the dog's tireless attack at a specific area of the body, almost always the legs or paws. The dog licks so intensively that he removes the hair and skin, leaving an ugly, large wound. Tiny protuberances, which are outgrowths of new capillaries, bead on the surface of the wound. Owners who notice their dogs' biting and chewing at their extremities should have the vet determine the cause. If lick granuloma is identified, although there is no absolute cure, corticosteroids are the most common treatment.

AIRBORNE ALLERGIES

An interesting allergy is pollen allergy. Humans have hay fever, rose fever and other fevers from which they suffer during the pollinating season. Many dogs suffer the same allergies. When the pollen count is high, your dog might suffer, but don't expect him to sneeze and have a runny nose like a human would. Dogs react to pollen allergies the same way they react to fleas—they scratch and bite themselves.

Dogs, like humans, can be tested for allergens. Discuss the testing with your veterinary dermatologist.

CARETAKER OF TEETH

You are your dog's caretaker and his dentist. Vets warn that plaque and tartar buildup on the teeth will damage the gums and allow bacteria to enter the dog's bloodstream, causing serious damage to the animal's vital organs. Studies show that over 50 percent of dogs have some form of gum disease before age three. Daily or weekly tooth cleaning (with a brush or soft gauze pad wipes) can add to your dog's life.

FOOD PROBLEMS

FOOD ALLERGIES

Dogs are allergic to many foods that are best-sellers and highly recommended by breeders and veterinary surgeons. Changing the brand of food that you buy may not eliminate the problem if the element to which the dog is allergic is contained in the new brand.

Recognising a food allergy is difficult. Humans vomit or have rashes when they eat a food to which they are allergic. Dogs neither vomit nor (usually) develop rashes. They react in the same manner as they would to an airborne or flea allergy; they itch, scratch and bite, thus making the diagnosis extremely difficult. While pollen allergies and parasite bites are usually seasonal, food allergies are year-round problems.

FOOD INTOLERANCE

Food intolerance is the inability of the dog to completely digest certain foods. For example, puppies that may have done very well on their mother's milk may not do well on cow's milk. The results of food intolerance may be evident in loose bowels, passing gas and stomach pains. These are the only obvious symptoms of food intolerance, which makes diagnosis difficult.

TREATING FOOD PROBLEMS

It is possible to handle food allergies and food intolerance yourself. Start by putting your dog on a diet that he has never had. Obviously, if the dog has never eaten this new food, he can't have been allergic or intolerant of it. Start with a single ingredient that is not in the dog's diet at the present time. Ingredients like chopped beef or fish are common in dogs' diets, so try something more exotic like rabbit, pheasant or even just vegetables. Keep the dog on this diet (with no additives) for a month. If the symptoms of food allergy or intolerance disappear, it is quite likely that your dog has a food allergy.

Don't think that the single ingredient cured the problem. You still must find a suitable diet and ascertain which ingredient in the old diet was objectionable. This is most easily done by adding ingredients to the new diet one at a time. Let the dog stay on the modified diet for a month before you add another ingredient. Eventually, you will determine the ingredient that caused the adverse reaction.

An alternative method is to carefully study the ingredients in the diet to which your dog is allergic or intolerant. Identify the main ingredient in this diet and eliminate the main ingredient by buying a different food that does not have that ingredient. Keep experimenting until the symptoms disappear after one month on the new diet.

EXTERNAL PARASITES

FLEAS

Of all the problems to which dogs
are prone, none is more well
known and frustrating than fleas.
Flea infestation is relatively simple
to cure but difficult to prevent.
Parasites that are harboured inside
the body are a bit more difficult to
eradicate but they are easier to
control.

Magnified head
of a dog flea,
*Ctenocephalides
canis.*

S. E. M. by Dr Dennis Kunkel, University of Hawaii

To control flea infestation, you
have to understand the flea's life
cycle. Fleas are often thought of as
a summertime problem, but
centrally heated homes have
changed the patterns and fleas can
be found at any time of the year.
The most effective method of flea
control is a two-stage approach:
one stage to kill the adult fleas,
and the other to control the
development of pre-adult fleas.
Unfortunately, no single active
ingredient is effective against all
stages of the life cycle.

LIFE CYCLE STAGES

During its life, a flea will pass
through four life stages: egg, larva,
pupa and adult. The adult stage is
the most visible and irritating stage
of the flea life cycle, and this is

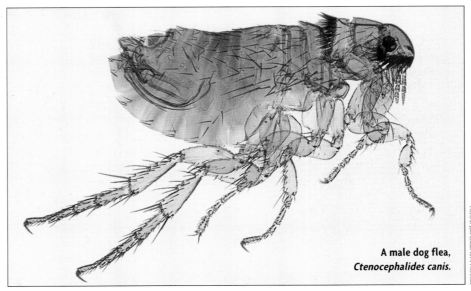

Opposite page:
A scanning
electron
micrograph of a
dog or cat flea,
Ctenocephalides,
magnified more
than 100x. This
image has been
colorized
for effect.

A male dog flea,
Ctenocephalides canis.

Photo by Jean Claude Revy/Phototake

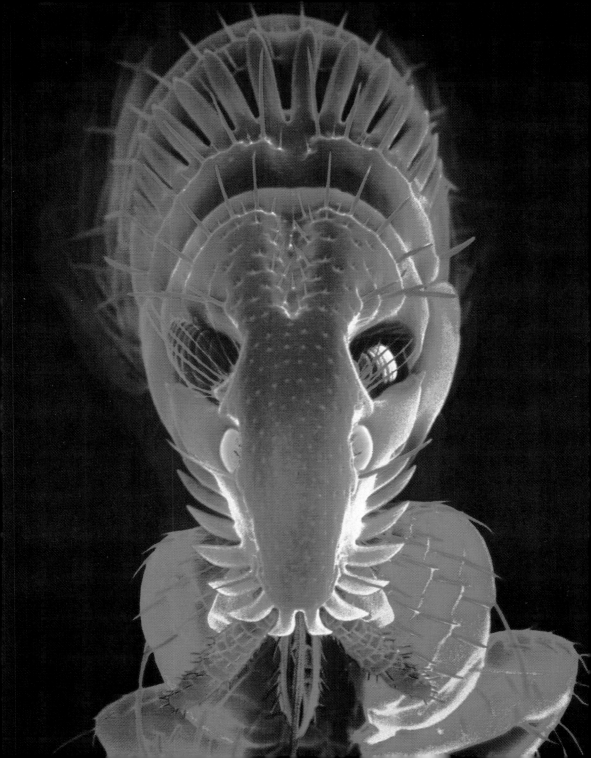

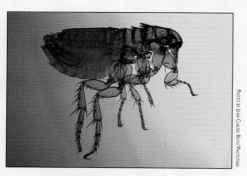

PHOTO BY JEAN CLAUDE REVY/PHOTOTAKE

A LOOK AT FLEAS

Fleas have been around for millions of years and have adapted to changing host animals. They are able to go through a complete life cycle in less than one month or they can extend their lives to almost two years by remaining as pupae or cocoons. They do not need blood or any other food for up to 20 months.

They have been measured as being able to jump 300,000 times and can jump 150 times their length in any direction, including straight up. Those are just a few of the reasons why they are so successful in infesting a dog!

why the majority of flea-control products concentrate on this stage. The fact is that adult fleas account for only 1% of the total flea population, and the other 99% exist in pre-adult stages, i.e. eggs, larvae and pupae. The pre-adult stages are barely visible to the naked eye.

THE LIFE CYCLE OF THE FLEA

Eggs are laid on the dog, usually in quantities of about 20 or 30, several times a day. The female adult flea must have a blood meal before each egg-laying session. When first laid, the eggs will cling to the dog's hair, as the eggs are still moist. However, they will quickly dry out and fall from the dog, especially if the dog moves around or scratches. Many eggs will fall off in the dog's favourite area or an area in which he spends a lot of time, such as his bed.

Once the eggs fall from the dog onto the carpet or furniture, they will hatch into larvae. This takes from one to ten days. Larvae are not particularly mobile and will usually travel only a few inches

The Life Cycle of the Flea

Eggs

Larvae

Pupa

Adult

Photos courtesy of Fleabusters'; Rx for fleas.

from where they hatch. However, they do have a tendency to move away from light and heavy traffic—under furniture and behind doors are common places to find high quantities of flea larvae.

The flea larvae feed on dead organic matter, including adult flea faeces, until they are ready to change into adult fleas. Fleas will usually remain as larvae for around seven days. After this period, the larvae will pupate into protective pupae. While inside the pupae, the larvae will undergo metamorphosis and change into adult fleas. This can take as little time as a few days, but the adult fleas can remain inside the pupae waiting to hatch for up to two years. The pupae are signalled to hatch by certain stimuli, such as physical pressure—the pupae's being stepped on, heat from an animal's lying on the pupae or increased carbon dioxide levels and vibrations—indicating that a suitable host is available.

FLEA KILLERS

Flea-killers are poisonous. You should not spray these toxic chemicals on areas of a dog's body that he licks, on his genitals or on his face. Flea killers taken internally are a better answer, but check with your vet in case internal therapy is not advised for your dog.

INSECT GROWTH REGULATOR (IGR)

Two types of products should be used when treating fleas—a product to treat the pet and a product to treat the home. Adult fleas represent less than 1% of the flea population. The pre-adult fleas (eggs, larvae and pupae) represent more than 99% of the flea population and are found in the environment; it is in the case of pre-adult fleas that products containing an Insect Growth Regulator (IGR) should be used in the home.

IGRs are a new class of compounds used to prevent the development of insects. They do not kill the insect outright, but instead use the insect's biology against it to stop it from completing its growth. Products that contain methoprene are the world's first and leading IGRs. Used to control fleas and other insects, this type of IGR will stop flea larvae from developing and protect the house for up to seven months.

Once hatched, the adult flea must feed within a few days. Once the adult flea finds a host, it will not leave voluntarily. It only becomes dislodged by grooming or the host animal's scratching. The adult flea will remain on the host for the duration of its life unless forcibly removed.

PHOTO BY DWIGHT R KUHN

Dwight R Kuhn's magnificent action photo, showing a flea jumping from a dog's back.

TREATING THE ENVIRONMENT AND THE DOG

Treating fleas should be a two-pronged attack. First, the environment needs to be treated; this includes carpets and furniture, especially the dog's bedding and areas underneath furniture. The environment should be treated with a household spray containing an Insect Growth Regulator (IGR) and an insecticide to kill the adult fleas. Most IGRs are effective against eggs and larvae; they

A scanning electron micrograph (S. E. M.) of a dog flea, *Ctenocephalides canis.*

S. E. M. BY DR DENNIS KUNKEL, UNIVERSITY OF HAWAII

actually mimic the fleas' own hormones and stop the eggs and larvae from developing into adult fleas. There are currently no treatments available to attack the pupa stage of the life cycle, so the adult insecticide is used to kill the newly hatched adult fleas before they find a host. Most IGRs are active for many months, while adult insecticides are only active for a few days.

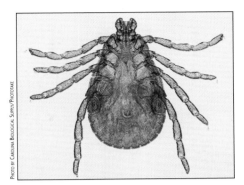

A brown dog tick, *Rhipicephalus sanguineus*, is an uncommon but annoying tick found on dogs.

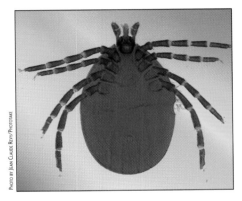

An uncommon dog tick of the genus *Ixode*. Magnified 10x.

When treating with a household spray, it is a good idea to vacuum before applying the product. This stimulates as many pupae as possible to hatch into adult fleas. The vacuum cleaner should also be treated with an insecticide to prevent the eggs and larvae that have been hoovered into the vacuum bag from hatching.

The second stage of treatment is to apply an adult insecticide to the dog. Traditionally, this would be in the form of a collar or a spray, but more recent innovations include digestible insecticides that poison the fleas when they ingest the dog's blood. Alternatively, there are drops that, when placed on the back of the animal's neck, spread throughout the fur and skin to kill adult fleas.

TICKS AND MITES

Though not as common as fleas, ticks and mites are found all over the tropical and temperate world. They don't bite, like fleas; they harpoon. They dig their sharp proboscis (nose) into the dog's skin and drink the blood. Their only food and drink is dog's blood. Dogs can get Lyme disease, Rocky Mountain spotted fever (normally found in the US only), paralysis and many other diseases from ticks and mites. They may live where fleas are

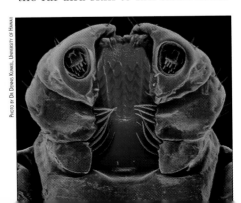

The head of a dog tick, *Dermacentor variabilis*, enlarged and coloured for effect.

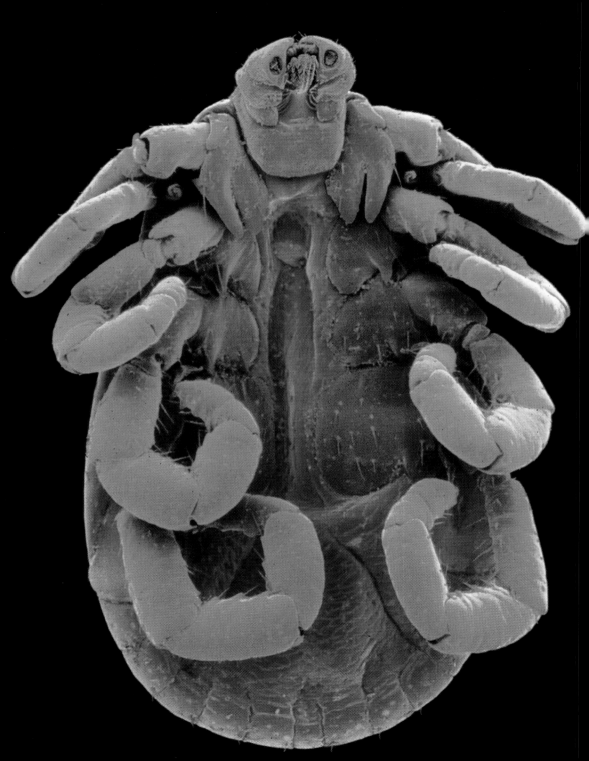

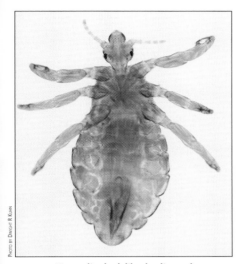

PHOTO BY DWIGHT R KUHN

Human lice look like dog lice and the two are closely related.

BEWARE THE DEER TICK

The great outdoors may be fun for your dog, but it also is a home to dangerous ticks. Deer ticks carry a bacterium known as *Borrelia burgdorferi* and are most active in the autumn and spring. When infections are caught early, penicillin and tetracycline are effective antibiotics, but if left untreated the bacteria may cause neurological, kidney and cardiac problems as well as long-term trouble with walking and painful joints.

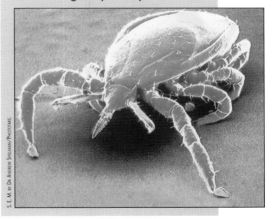

S. E. M. BY DR ANDREW SPIELMAN/PHOTOTAKE.

found and they like to hide in cracks or seams in walls wherever dogs live. They are controlled the same way fleas are controlled.

The dog tick, *Dermacentor variabilis*, may well be the most common dog tick in many geographical areas, especially those areas where the climate is hot and humid.

Most dog ticks have life expectancies of a week to six months, depending upon climatic conditions. They can neither jump nor fly, but they

Opposite page:
The dog tick, *Dermacentor variabilis*, is probably the most common tick found on dogs. Look at the strength in its eight legs! No wonder it's hard to detach them.

can crawl slowly and can range up to 5 metres (16 feet) to reach a sleeping or unsuspecting dog.

MANGE

Mites cause a skin irritation called mange. Some are contagious, like *Cheyletiella*, ear mites, scabies and chiggers. Mites that cause ear-mite infestations are usually controlled with Lindane, which can only be

The mange mite, *Psoroptes bovis.*

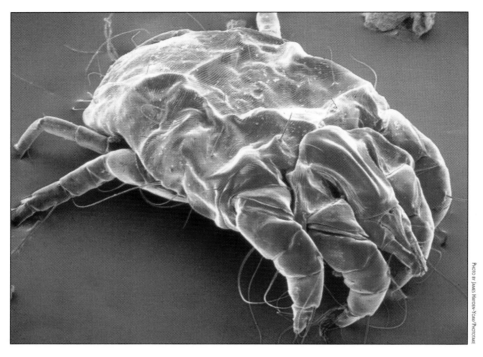

PHOTO BY JAMES HAYDEN-YOAV/PHOTOTAKE

The roundworm, *Rhabditis.* The roundworm can infect both dogs and humans.

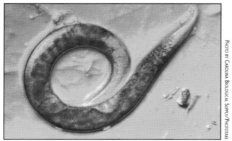

PHOTO BY CAROLINA BIOLOGICAL SUPPLY/PHOTOTAKE

The common roundworm, *Ascaris lumbricoides.*

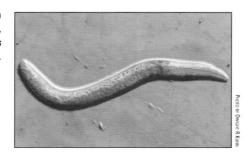

PHOTO BY DWIGHT R KUHN

administered by a vet, followed by Tresaderm at home.

It is essential that your dog be treated for mange as quickly as possible because some forms of mange are transmissible to people.

INTERNAL PARASITES

Most animals—fishes, birds and mammals, including dogs and humans—have worms and other parasites that live inside their bodies. According to Dr Herbert R Axelrod, the fish pathologist, there are two kinds of parasites: dumb and smart. The smart parasites live in peaceful cooperation with their hosts (symbiosis), while the dumb parasites kill their hosts. Most of the worm infections are relatively easy to control. If they are not controlled, they weaken the host dog to the point that other medical problems occur, but they are not dumb parasites.

ROUNDWORMS

The roundworms that infect dogs are scientifically known as *Toxocara canis*. They live in the dog's intestines. The worms shed eggs continually. It has been estimated that a dog produces about 150 grammes of faeces every day. Each gramme of faeces

ROUNDWORMS

Average size dogs can pass 1,360,000 roundworm eggs every day. For example, if there were only 1 million dogs in the world, the world would be saturated with 1,300 metric tonnes of dog faeces. These faeces would contain 15,000,000,000 roundworm eggs.

Up to 31% of home gardens and children's play boxes in the US contain roundworm eggs.

Flushing dog's faeces down the toilet is not a safe practice because the usual sewage treatments do not destroy roundworm eggs.

Infected puppies start shedding roundworm eggs at 3 weeks of age. They can be infected by their mother's milk.

DEWORMING

Ridding your puppy of worms is *very important* because certain worms that puppies carry, such as tapeworms and roundworms, can infect humans.

Breeders initiate deworming programmes at or about four weeks of age. The routine is repeated every two or three weeks until the puppy is three months old. The breeder from whom you obtained your puppy should provide you with the complete details of the deworming programme.

Your veterinary surgeon can prescribe and monitor the programme of deworming for you. The usual programme is treating the puppy every 15–20 days until the puppy is positively worm-free. It is advised that you only treat your puppy with drugs that are recommended professionally.

averages 10,000–12,000 eggs of roundworms. There are no known areas in which dogs roam that do not contain roundworm eggs. The greatest danger of roundworms is that they infect people too! It is wise to have your dog tested regularly for roundworms.

Pigs also have roundworm infections that can be passed to humans and dogs. The typical roundworm parasite is called *Ascaris lumbricoides*.

Left: The roundworm *Rhabditis*. Right: Male and female hookworms. *Ancylostoma caninum* are uncommonly found in pet or show dogs in Britain.

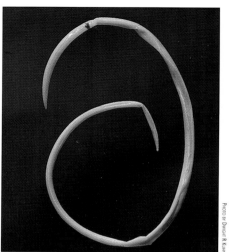

HOOKWORMS

The worm *Ancylostoma caninum* is commonly called the dog hookworm. It is also dangerous to humans and cats. It has teeth by which it attaches itself to the intestines of the dog. It changes the site of its attachment about six times a day and the dog loses blood from each detachment, possibly causing iron-deficiency anaemia. Hookworms are easily purged from the dog with many medications. Milbemycin oxime, which also serves as a heartworm

The infective stage of the hookworm larva.

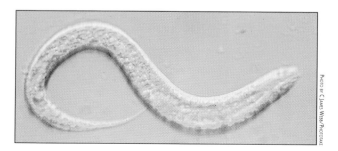

preventative in Collies, can be used for this purpose.

In Britain the 'temperate climate' hookworm (*Uncinaria stenocephala*) is rarely found in pet or show dogs, but can occur in hunting packs, racing Greyhounds and sheepdogs because the worms can be prevalent wherever dogs are exercised regularly on grassland.

TAPEWORMS

There are many species of tapeworm. They are carried by fleas! The dog eats the flea and starts the tapeworm cycle. Humans can also be infected with tapeworms, so don't eat fleas! Fleas are so small that your dog could pass them onto your hands, your plate or your food and thus make it possible for you to ingest a flea that is carrying tapeworm eggs.

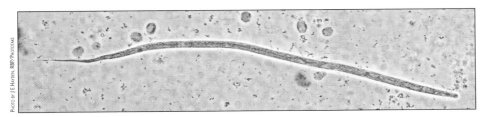

Heartworm,
Dirofilaria immitis.

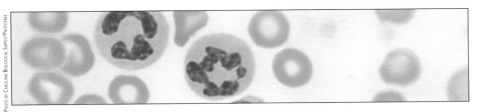

Magnified
heartworm larvae,
Dirofilaria immitis.

While tapeworm infection is not life-threatening in dogs (smart parasite!), it can be the cause of a very serious liver disease for humans.

About 50 percent of the humans infected with *Echinococcus multilocularis*, a type of tapeworm that causes alveolar hydatis, perish.

TAPEWORMS

Humans, rats, squirrels, foxes, coyotes, wolves, wolves and domestic dogs dogs are all susceptible to tapeworm infection. Except in humans, tapeworms are usually not a fatal infection. Infected individuals can harbour a thousand parasitic worms.

Tapeworms have two sexes—male and female (many other worms have only one sex—male and female in the same worm).

If dogs eat infected rats or mice, they get the tapeworm disease. One month after attaching to a dog's intestine, the worm starts shedding eggs. These eggs are infective immediately. Infective eggs can live for a few months without a host animal.

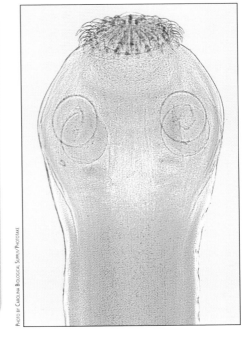

The head and rostellum (the round prominence on the scolex) of a tapeworm, which infects dogs and humans.

The heart of a dog infected with canine heartworm, *Dirofilaria immitis.*

HEARTWORMS

Heartworms are thin, extended worms up to 30 cms (12 ins) long, which live in a dog's heart and the major blood vessels surrounding it. Dogs may have up to 200 worms. Symptoms may be loss of energy, loss of appetite, coughing, the development of a pot belly and anaemia.

Heartworms are transmitted by mosquitoes. The mosquito drinks the blood of an infected dog and takes in larvae with the blood. The larvae, called microfilaria, develop within the body of the mosquito and are passed on to the next dog bitten after the larvae mature. It takes two to three weeks for the larvae to develop to the infective stage within the body of the mosquito. Dogs should be treated at about six weeks of age, and maintained on a prophylactic dose given monthly.

Blood testing for heartworms is not necessarily indicative of how seriously your dog is infected. This is a dangerous disease. Although heartworm is a problem for dogs in America, Australia, Asia and Central Europe, dogs in the United Kingdom are not currently affected by heartworm.

First Aid at a Glance

Burns
Place the affected area under cool water; use ice if only a small area is burnt.

Bee/Insect bites
Apply ice to relieve swelling; antihistamine dosed properly.

Animal bites
Clean any bleeding area; apply pressure until bleeding subsides; go to the vet.

Spider bites
Use cold compress and a pressurised pack to inhibit venom's spreading.

Antifreeze poisoning
Induce vomiting with hydrogen peroxide. Seek *immediate* veterinary help!

Fish hooks
Removal best handled by vet; hook must be cut in order to remove.

Snake bites
Pack ice around bite; contact vet quickly; identify snake for proper antivenin.

Car accident
Move dog from roadway with blanket; seek veterinary aid.

Shock
Calm the dog, keep him warm; seek immediate veterinary help.

Nosebleed
Apply cold compress to the nose; apply pressure to any visible abrasion.

Bleeding
Apply pressure above the area; treat wound by applying a cotton pack.

Heat stroke
Submerge dog in cold bath; cool down with fresh air and water; go to the vet.

Frostbite/Hypothermia
Warm the dog with a warm bath, electric blankets or hot water bottles.

Abrasions
Clean the wound and wash out thoroughly with fresh water; apply antiseptic.

 Remember: an injured dog may attempt to bite a helping hand from fear and confusion. Always muzzle the dog before trying to offer assistance.

In the show ring, the Pyrenean sparkles as a snow-white beauty whose days of tackling wolves seem far behind him.

PYRENEAN MOUNTAIN DOG

When you purchase your Pyrenean Mountain Dog, you will make it clear to the breeder whether you want one just as a loveable companion and pet, or if you hope to be buying a Pyrenean with show prospects. No reputable breeder will sell you a young puppy and tell you that it is *definitely* of show quality, for so much can go wrong during the early months of a puppy's development. If you plan to show, what you will hopefully have acquired is a puppy with 'show potential.'

To the novice, exhibiting a Pyrenean Mountain Dog in the show ring may look easy, but it takes a lot of hard work and devotion to do top winning at a show such as the prestigious Crufts Dog Show, not to mention a little luck too!

The first concept that the canine novice learns when watching a dog show is that each dog first competes against members of its own breed. Once the judge has selected the best member of each breed (Best of Breed), provided that the show is judged on a Group system, that

chosen dog will compete with other dogs in its group. Finally, the best of each group will compete for Best in Show and Reserve Best in Show.

The second concept that you must understand is that the dogs are not actually compared against one another. The judge compares each dog against its breed standard, which is a written description of the ideal specimen of the breed. While some early

Exhibiting a Pyrenean Mountain Dog in top condition requires dedication, training and financial commitment.

breed standards were indeed based on specific dogs that were famous or popular, many dedicated enthusiasts say that a perfect specimen, as described in the standard, has never walked

into a show ring, has never been bred and, to the woe of dog breeders around the globe, does not exist. Breeders attempt to get as close to this ideal as possible with every litter, but theoretically the 'perfect' dog is so elusive that it is impossible. (And if the 'perfect' dog were born, breeders and judges would never agree that it was indeed 'perfect.')

If you are interested in exploring the world of dog showing, your best bet is to join your local breed club. These clubs often host both Championship and Open Shows, and sometimes Match meetings and special events, all of which could be of interest, even if you are only an onlooker. Clubs also send out newsletters, and some organise training days and seminars in order that interested people may learn more about their chosen breed. To locate the breed club closest to you, contact The Kennel Club, the ruling body for the British dog world.

The Kennel Club governs not only conformation shows but also working trials, obedience, agility trials and field trials. The Kennel Club furnishes the rules and regulations for all of these events plus general dog registration and other basic requirements of dog ownership. Its annual show, called the Crufts Dog Show, held in Birmingham, is the largest benched show in England. Every

A GENTLEMAN'S SPORT

Whether or not your dog wins top honours, showing is a pleasant social event. Sometimes, one may meet a troublemaker or nasty exhibitor, but these people should be ignored and forgotten. In the extremely rare case that someone threatens or harasses you or your dog, you can lodge a complaint with The Kennel Club. This should be done with extreme prudence. Complaints are investigated seriously and should never be filed on a whim.

year over 20,000 of the UK's best dogs qualify to participate in this marvellous show, which lasts four days.

The Kennel Club governs many different kinds of shows in Great Britain, Australia, South Africa and beyond. At the most competitive and prestigious of these shows, the Championship Shows, a dog can earn Challenge Certificates (CCs), and thereby become a Show Champion or a Champion. A dog must earn three Challenge Certificates under three different judges to earn the prefix of 'Sh Ch' or 'Ch.' Some breeds must also qualify in a field trial in order to gain the title of full Champion, though the Pyrenean is not one such breed. Challenge Certificates are awarded to a very small percentage of the dogs competing, and dogs that are

Presentation is half the battle at a dog show. Not only must you show your majestic Mountain Dog to his best advantage, you must present yourself as a well-prepared professional.

already Champions compete with others for these coveted CCs. The number of Challenge Certificates awarded in any one year is based upon the total number of dogs in each breed entered for competition.

There are three types of Championship Shows: an all-breed General Championship Show for all Kennel-Club-recognised breeds; a Group Championship Show, which is limited to breeds within one of the groups; and a Breed Show, which is usually confined to a single breed. The Kennel Club determines which breeds at which Championship Shows will have the opportunity to earn Challenge Certificates (or tickets). Serious exhibitors often will opt not to participate if the tickets are withheld at a particular show. This policy makes earning

WINNING THE TICKET

Earning a championship at Kennel Club shows is the most difficult in the world. Compared to the United States and Canada, where it is relatively not 'challenging,' collecting three green tickets not only requires much time and effort, it can be very expensive! Challenge Certificates, as the tickets are properly known, are the building blocks of champions—good breeding, good handling, good training and good luck!

championships even more difficult to accomplish.

Open Shows are generally less competitive and are frequently used as 'practice shows' for young dogs. There are hundreds of Open Shows each year that can be delightful social events and are great first show experiences for the novice. Even if you're considering just watching a show to wet your paws, an Open Show is a great choice.

While Championship and Open Shows are most important for the beginner to understand, there are other types of shows in which the interested dog owner can participate. Training clubs sponsor Matches that can be entered on the day of the show for a nominal fee. In these introductory-level exhibitions, two dogs' names are pulled out of a hat and 'matched,' the winner of that match goes on to the next round and eventually only one dog is left undefeated.

Exemption Shows are much more light-hearted affairs with usually only four pedigree classes and several 'fun' classes, all of which can be entered on the day of the show. Exemption Shows are sometimes held in conjunction with small agricultural shows and the proceeds must be given to a charity. Limited Shows are also available in small number. Entry is restricted to members of the club that hosts the show, although

SHOW QUALITY SHOWS
While you may purchase a puppy in the hope of having a successful career in the show ring, it is impossible to tell, at eight to ten weeks of age, whether your dog will be a contender. Some promising pups end up with minor to serious faults that prevent them from taking home a Best of Breed award, but this certainly does not mean they can't be the best of companions for you and your family. To find out if your potential show dog is show quality, enter him in a match to see how a judge evaluates him. You may also take him back to your breeder as the pup matures to see what he might advise.

one can usually join the club when making an entry.

Before you actually step into the ring, you would be well advised to sit back and observe the judge's ring procedure. If it is your first time in the ring, do not be over-anxious and run to the front of the line. It is much better to stand back and study how the exhibitor in front of you is performing. The judge asks each handler to 'stand' the dog, hopefully showing the dog off to his best advantage. The judge will observe the dog from a distance and from different angles, and approach the dog to check his teeth, testicles, overall structure, alertness and muscle tone, as well as consider how well the dog 'conforms' to the standard. Most importantly, the judge will have the exhibitor move the dog around the ring in some pattern that he or she should specify (another advantage to not going first, but always listen since some judges change their directions—and the judge is always right!). Finally, the judge will give the dog one last look before moving on to the next exhibitor.

If you are not in the top three at your first show, do not be discouraged. Be patient and consistent, and you may eventually find yourself in the winning line-up. Remember that the winners were once in your shoes and have devoted many hours and much money to earn the placement. If you find that your dog is losing every time and never getting a nod, it may be time to consider a different dog sport or to just enjoy your Pyrenean as a pet.

Virtually all countries with a recognised speciality breed club (sometimes called a 'parent' club) offer show conformation competition specifically for and among Pyrenean Mountain Dogs. Under direction of the club, other special events for obedience, agility, carting and testing other breed-specific instincts may be offered as well, whether for titling or just for fun.

WORKING TRIALS

Working trials can be entered by any well-trained dog of any breed, not just Gundogs or Working dogs. Many dogs that earn the Kennel Club Good Citizen Dog award choose to participate in a working trial. There are five stakes at both Open and Championship levels: Companion Dog (CD), Utility Dog (UD), Working Dog (WD), Tracking Dog (TD) and Patrol Dog (PD). As in conformation shows, dogs compete against a standard and, if the dog reaches the qualifying mark, it obtains a certificate. The exercises are divided into groups, and the dog must achieve at least 70 percent of the allotted score for each exercise in order to qualify. If the dog achieves 80 percent in the Open level, it receives a Certificate of Merit (COM); in the Championship level, it receives a Qualifying Certificate. At the CD stake, dogs must participate in four groups: Control, Stay, Agility and Search (Retrieve and

If it is your first time in the show ring, you are well advised to observe how the handlers in the ring are conducting themselves.

Nosework). At the next three levels, UD, WD and TD, there are only three groups: Control, Agility and Nosework.

The Agility exercises consist of three jumps: a vertical scale up a six-foot wall of planks; a clear jump over a basic three-foot hurdle with a removable top bar; and a long jump across angled planks stretching nine feet.

To earn the UD, WD and TD, dogs must track approximately one-half mile for articles laid from one-half hour to three hours previously. Tracks consist of turns and legs, and fresh ground is used for each participant. The fifth stake, PD, involves teaching manwork, which is not recommended for every breed.

AGILITY TRIALS

Agility trials began in the United Kingdom in 1977 and have since spread around the world, especially to the United States, where they are very popular. The handler directs his dog over an obstacle course that includes jumps (such as those used in the working trials), as well as tyres, the dog walk, weave poles, pipe tunnels, collapsed tunnels, etc. The Kennel Club requires that dogs not be trained for agility until they are 12 months old. This dog sport is great fun for dog and owner, and interested owners should join a training club that has obstacles and

experienced agility handlers who can introduce you and your dog to the 'ropes' (and tyres, tunnels, etc.).

FÉDÉRATION CYNOLOGIQUE INTERNATIONALE

Established in 1911, the Fédération Cynologique Internationale (FCI) represents the 'world kennel club.' This international body brings uniformity to the breeding, judging and showing of pure-bred dogs. Although the FCI originally included only five European nations: France, Germany, Austria, the Netherlands and Belgium (which remains its headquarters), the organisation today embraces nations on six continents and recognises well over 300 breeds of pure-bred dog.

FCI INFORMATION

There are 330 breeds recognised by the FCI, and each breed is considered to be 'owned' by a specific country. Each breed standard is a cooperative effort between the breed's country and the FCI's Standards and Scientific Commissions. Judges use these official breed standards at shows held in FCI member countries. One of the functions of the FCI is to update and translate the breed standards into French, English, Spanish and German.

FCI sponsors both national and international shows. The hosting country determines the judging system and breed standards are always based on the breed's country of origin. Dogs from every country can participate in these impressive canine spectacles, the largest of which is the World Dog Show, hosted in a different country each year.

There are three titles attainable through the FCI: the International Champion, which is the most prestigious; the International Beauty Champion, which is based on aptitude certificates in different countries; and the International Trial Champion, which is based on achievement in obedience trials in different countries.

The top award in an FCI show is the CAC (*Certificats d'Aptitude au Championnat*) and to gain a championship, a dog must win three CACs at regional or club shows under three different judges who are breed specialists. The title of International Champion is gained by winning four CACIBs (*Certificat d'Aptitude au Championnat International de Beauté*), which are offered only at international shows, with at least a one-year lapse between the first and fourth award.

The FCI is divided into ten 'Groups.' At the World Dog Show, the following 'Classes' are offered for each breed: Puppy Class (6–9

Pyreneans and their handlers in the breed ring, awaiting a look from the judge.

months), Youth Class (9–18 months), Open Class (15 months or older) and Champion Class. A dog can be awarded a classification of Excellent, Very Good, Good, Sufficient and Not Sufficient. Puppies can be awarded classifications of Very Promising, Promising or Not Promising. Four placements are made in each class. After all classes are judged, a Best of Breed is selected. Other special groups and classes may also be shown. Each exhibitor showing a dog receives a written evaluation from the judge.

Besides the World Dog Show and other all-breed shows, you can exhibit your dog at speciality shows held by different breed clubs. Speciality shows may have their own regulations.

PYRENEAN MOUNTAIN DOG

The term *old* is a qualitative term. For dogs, as well as for their masters, old is relative. Certainly we can all distinguish between a puppy Pyrenean Mountain Dog and an adult Pyrenean Mountain Dog—there are the obvious physical traits, such as size, appearance and facial expressions, and personality traits. Puppies and young dogs like to play with children. Children's natural exuberance is a good match for the seemingly endless energy of young dogs. They like to run, jump and play. When dogs grow older and cease their interaction with children, they are often thought of as being too old to keep pace with the children. On the other hand, if a Pyrenean is only exposed to older people or quieter lifestyles, his life will normally be less active and the decrease in his activity level as he ages will not be as obvious.

If people live to be 100 years old, dogs live to be 20 years old. While this might seem like a good rule of thumb, it is very inaccurate. When trying to compare dog years to human years, you cannot make a generalisation about all dogs. In the

Changes in a senior dog can be rather subtle, especially on a white and grey dog, where the telltale greying muzzle will be difficult to detect.

Pyrenean Mountain Dog, lifespan for a male averages 10–12 years, but bitches seem to average 10–13 years. However, there can, of course, be exceptions.

Dogs generally are considered physically mature at around three years of age (or earlier), but can reproduce even earlier. So the first three years of a dog's life are like seven times that of comparable humans. That means a 3-year-old dog is like a 21-year-old human. However, as the curve of comparison shows, there is no hard and fast rule for comparing dog and human ages. Small breeds tend to live longer than many large breeds, some breeds' adolescent periods last

For the purposes of feeding and veterinary care, six or seven years is the age when most Pyrenean Mountain Dog breeders consider the dog to be a senior or veteran.

longer than others' and some breeds experience rapid periods of growth. The comparison is made even more difficult, for, likewise, not all humans age at the same rate...and human females live longer than human males.

WHAT TO LOOK FOR IN SENIORS

Most veterinary surgeons and behaviourists use the seven-year mark as the time to consider a dog a 'senior.' The term 'senior' does not imply that the dog is geriatric and has begun to fail in mind and body. Ageing is essentially a

Some Pyrs are lazy years before they're old!

> ### GETTING OLD
> The bottom line is simply that your dog is getting old when YOU think he is getting old because he slows down in his level of general activity, including walking, running, eating, jumping and retrieving. On the other hand, the frequency of certain activities increases, such as more sleeping, more barking and more repetition of habits like going to the door without being called when you put your coat on to leave the house.

slowing process. Humans readily admit that they feel a difference in their activity level from age 20 to 30, and then from 30 to 40, etc. By treating the seven-year-old dog as a senior, owners are able to implement certain therapeutic and preventative medical strategies with the help of their veterinary surgeons. A senior-care programme should include at least two veterinary visits per year and screening sessions to determine the dog's health status, as well as nutritional counselling. Veterinary surgeons determine the senior dog's health status through a blood smear for a complete blood count, serum chemistry profile with electrolytes, urinalysis, blood pressure check, electrocardiogram, ocular tonometry (pressure on the eyeball) and dental prophylaxis.

Such an extensive programme for senior dogs is well advised

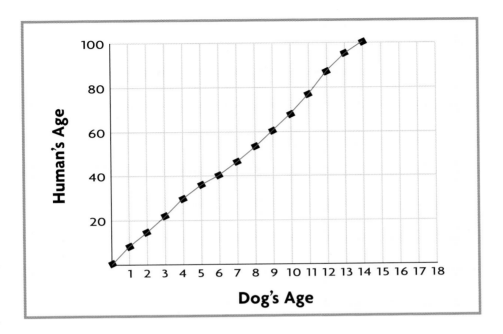

before owners start to see the obvious physical signs of ageing, such as slower and inhibited

CONSISTENCY COUNTS

Puppies and older dogs are very similar in their need for consistency in their lives. Older pets may experience hearing and vision loss, or may just be more easily confused by changes in their homes. Try to keep things consistent for the senior dog. For example, doors that are always open or closed should remain so. Most importantly, don't dismiss a pet just because he's getting old; most senior dogs remain active and important parts of their owners' lives.

movement, greying, increased sleep/nap periods and disinterest in play and other activity. This preventative programme promises a longer, healthier life for the ageing dog. Among the physical problems common in ageing dogs are the loss of sight and hearing, arthritis, kidney and liver failure, diabetes mellitus, heart disease and Cushing's disease (an hormonal disease).

In addition to the physical manifestations discussed, there are some behavioural changes and problems related to ageing dogs. Dogs suffering from hearing or vision loss, dental discomfort or arthritis can become aggressive. Likewise, the near-deaf and/or blind dog may be startled more easily and react in an unexpectedly aggressive manner. Seniors suffering from senility can become more impatient and irritable. Housesoiling accidents are associated with loss of mobility, kidney problems and loss of sphincter control as well as plaque accumulation, physiological brain changes and reactions to medications. Older dogs, just like young puppies, suffer from separation anxiety, which can lead to excessive barking, whining, housesoiling and destructive behaviour. Seniors may become fearful of everyday sounds, such as vacuum cleaners, heaters, thunder and passing traffic. Some dogs have difficulty sleeping, due to discomfort, the need for frequent toilet visits and the like.

Owners should avoid spoiling the older dog with too many fatty treats. Obesity is a common problem in older dogs and subtracts years from their lives. Keep the senior dog as trim as possible, since excessive weight puts additional stress on the body's vital organs. Some breeders recommend supplementing the diet with foods high in fibre and lower in calories. Adding fresh vegetables and marrow broth to the senior's diet makes a tasty, low-calorie, low-fat supplement. Vets also offer speciality diets for senior dogs that are worth exploring.

Your dog, as he nears his twilight years, needs your patience and good care more than ever. Never punish an older dog for an accident or abnormal behaviour. For all the years of love, protection and companionship that your dog has provided, he deserves special attention and courtesies. The older dog may need to relieve himself at 3 a.m. because he can no longer hold it for eight hours. Older dogs may not be able to remain crated for more than two or three hours. It may be time to give up a sofa or chair to your old friend. Although he may not seem as enthusiastic about your attention and petting, he does appreciate the considerations you offer as he gets older.

Your Pyrenean Mountain Dog does not understand why his world is slowing down. Owners must make their dogs' transition into their golden years as pleasant and rewarding as possible.

WHAT TO DO WHEN THE TIME COMES

You are never fully prepared to make a rational decision about putting your dog to sleep. It is very obvious that you love your Pyrenean Mountain Dog or you would not be reading this book. Putting a beloved dog to sleep is extremely difficult. It is a decision that must be made with your veterinary surgeon. You are usually forced to make the decision when your dog experiences one or more life-threatening symptoms that have become serious enough for you to seek medical (veterinary) help.

If the prognosis of the malady indicates that the end is near and that your beloved pet will only continue to suffer and experience no enjoyment for the balance of its life, then euthanasia is the right choice.

WHAT IS EUTHANASIA?

Euthanasia derives from the Greek, meaning 'good death.' In other words, it means the planned, painless killing of a dog suffering from a painful, incurable condition, or who is so aged that it cannot walk, see, eat or control its excretory functions. Euthanasia is usually accomplished by injection with an overdose of anaesthesia or a barbiturate. Aside from the

Keep your senior dog in the best possible condition by adjusting his diet, exercise routine and the frequency of his veterinary visits.

prick of the needle, the experience is usually painless.

MAKING THE DECISION

The decision to euthanise your dog is never easy. The days during which the dog becomes ill and the end occurs can be unusually stressful for you. If this is your first experience with the death of a loved one, you may need the comfort dictated by your religious beliefs. If you are the head of the family and have children, you should have involved them in the decision of putting your Pyrenean Mountain Dog to sleep. Usually your dog can be maintained on drugs for a few days in order to give you ample time to make a decision. During this time, talking with members of your family or with people who have lived through the same experience can ease the burden of your inevitable decision.

THE FINAL RESTING PLACE

Dogs can have some of the same privileges as humans. The

In most pet cemeteries there are special areas in which your dog's ashes can be stored. The urns are usually available at the crematorium.

> **EUTHANASIA**
> Euthanasia must be performed by a licensed veterinary surgeon. There also may be societies for the prevention of cruelty to animals in your area. They often offer this service upon a vet's recommendation.

remains of your beloved dog can be buried in a pet cemetery, which is generally expensive. Dogs who have died at home can be buried in your garden in a place suitably marked with some stone or newly planted tree or bush. Alternatively, your dog can be cremated individually and the ashes returned to you. A less expensive option is mass cremation, although, of course, the ashes cannot then be returned. Vets can usually arrange the cremation on your behalf. The cost of these options should always be discussed frankly and openly with your veterinary surgeon. In Britain, if your dog has died at the surgery, the vet legally cannot allow you to take your dog's body home.

GETTING ANOTHER DOG?

The grief of losing your beloved dog will be as lasting as the grief of losing a human friend or relative. In most cases, if your dog died of old age (if there is

Most population centres have cemeteries in which pets can be buried. Discuss burial options with your vet.

such a thing), it had slowed down considerably. Do you want a new Pyrenean puppy to replace it? Or are you better off finding a mature Pyrenean Mountain Dog, say two to three years of age, which will usually

AGEING ADDITIVES

An healthy diet is important for dogs of all ages, but older dogs may benefit from the addition of supplements like antioxidants, which fight the ageing process, and vitamin B, which aids the kidneys. Check with your vet before adding these or any supplements to your pet's diet.

be house-trained and will have an already developed person-ality. In this case, you can find out if you like each other after a few hours of being together.

The decision is, of course, your own. Do you want another Pyrenean Mountain Dog or perhaps a different breed so as to avoid comparison with your beloved friend? Most people usually buy the same breed because they know (and love) the characteristics of that breed. Then, too, they often know people who have the same breed and perhaps they are lucky enough that one of their friends expects a litter soon. What could be better?

INDEX

My Pyrenean Mountain Dog

PUT YOUR PUPPY'S FIRST PICTURE HERE

Dog's Name _____

Date _____ Photographer _____